CONFLICT
AND
CONFLICT
RESOLUTION

A Sociological Introduction with Updated Bibliography and Theory Section

JACK NUSAN PORTER and RUTH TAPLIN

UNIVERSITY
PRESS OF
AMERICA

Lanham • New York • London

Copyright © 1987 by

University Press of America,® Inc.

4720 Boston Way
Lanham, MD 20706

3 Henrietta Street
London WC2E 8LU England

Printed in the United States of America

British Cataloging in Publication Information Available

Library of Congress Cataloging-in-Publication Data

Porter, Jack Nusan.
   Conflict and conflict resolution.

   Bibliography: p.
   1. Social conflict.   2. Conflict management.
3. Interpersonal conflict.   I. Taplin, Ruth.
II. Title.
HM136.P78   1987   303.6   87-8215
ISBN 0-8191-6368-6 (alk. paper)
ISBN 0-8191-6369-4 (pbk. : alk. paper)

All University Press of America books are produced on acid-free
paper which exceeds the minimum standards set by the National
Historical Publication and Records Commission.

Table of Contents

Acknowledgements

From JNP—

Dedicated to my teachers and colleagues at the University of Wisconsin-Milwaukee (1963–1967) and Northwestern University (1967–1971); and—

To the late Don Martindale whose wit, humor, and erudition were a model for all sociologists to follow. His famous textbook was a useful guide through the conflictual maze.

To my sociology professors at the University of Wisconsin and Northwestern University: Janet Abu-Lughod, Lakshmi Bharadwaj, Bernie Beck, Howard S. Becker, Karl Flaming, Scott Greer, Ray Mack, Charles Moskos, J. J. Palen, Allan Schnaiberg, Walter Wallace, the late Robert Winch, and especially Irwin Rinder for interesting me in the topic in the first place and to Jack Sawyer, Joe Blake, and Wen Lung Chang for their advice and generosity.

To Abby Solomon for her superb editing.

To Nikki Lewy, Linda Rosenthal, and Kathy Mendelson for their fine typing.

To my wife Miriam Almuly and our children Gabriel and Danielle for their patience and love. This book took longer than I thought, eighteen years too long.

Introduction

Conflict is the struggle over values or claims to status, power, and scarce resources, in which the aims of the groups or individuals involved are not only to obtain the desired values, but to also neutralize, injure, or eliminate rivals. This is the definition put forward by Lewis Coser in his *Continuities in the Study of Social Conflict* (1967). As Anthony Oberschall (1978) notes, social conflict is one of the most ubiquitous of events and encompasses a broad range of phenomena, including class, racial, religious, and community conflicts plus riots, rebellions, revolutions, strikes, marches, demonstrations, and protest rallies.

The focus of this short book is conflict and conflict resolution, in particular third-party mediation and reconciliation of conflict. We will explore the parameters of such resolution, but first, it is essential to examine the nature of conflict itself. An understanding of the means of conflict resolution entails an understanding of the procedures, functions, and toleration levels of conflict. To understand conciliation, it is imperative to understand the feud. Consequently, the works of the so-called "conflict theorists" will be cited: Simmel, Coser, Dahrendorf, and Gluckman.

Since mediation is essentially a situational phenomenon, the works of Erving Goffman, W. I. Thomas, and Georg Simmel will be discussed in this book plus we will emphasize a micro-structural approach rather than a macro-structural one. Necessarily such figures as Karl Marx, George Sorel, and the neo-Machiavellians (Pareto, Mosca, and Michels) will be excluded from this discussion because of reasons of space and relevance. It must be emphasized that this book is not concerned with *all* forms of conflict. To introduce discussions of class cohesion through conflict, class conflict, and revolution would divert attention from the central focus of this short book which is: the nature of conflict and its resolution in small-scale triadic interactions.

The sociology of conflict is a complex, multi-faceted field and there are many approaches at various levels of analysis. This book is only one modest approach.

Small group research has introduced new approaches to the area of conflict resolution. Social psychologists such as Bavelas, Borgatta, Newcomb, and Bales, have contributed to our general knowledge of problem-solving in small groups. Sociologists Theodore Caplow and Theodore Mills, for example, have focused upon communication and coalition formation in interpersonal triads. These face-to-face encounters are conceived as conflict-solving situations. They usually have three major functions: *communication:* through exchange of information, members of the triad arrive at a common definition of the situations they confront; *evaluation:* through exchange of ideas and opinions, guided by a mediator, they arrive at a shared consensus of attitudes toward the situation; and *control:* in the course of competing alternatives, the parties, again with the aid of the mediator, must choose and decide upon a course of action acceptable to all.

After the theoretical descriptions of conflict, situational theory, and small groups have been presented, the issue of conflict resolution will be developed through the use of a schema which describes the various types of such resolution. Mediation (conflict resolution) provides a link between disharmony and consensus and between conflict and conciliation.

After a discussion of various means of conflict resolution, the focus will then center upon what I call the *TMT* (Triadic Mediation Transaction), the situational transaction that occurs when a third party (the mediator or middleman) conciliates two opposing parties until consensus and/or compromise is reached. The role and function of the mediator will be explored as well as the protocol and ethics of the mediation.

And finally, the communication matrix of strategy and compromise will be explored through the use of game theory. Originally developed in 1944 by John Von Neumann and Oskar Morgenstern in their *Theory of Games and Economic Behavior,* game theory has seen widespread usage and application. In recent years, a body of literature has developed to show how game theory can be applied to "real-world" problems of conflict and their resolution. The works of Raiffa, Schelling, Luce, Buckley, and especially Boulding and Rapoport have been major contributions to the literature. Game theory's essential ideas, applications, and its limitations will be reviewed here. Whether game theoretical strategies may be properly applied to social behavior such as *TMT*s, both normatively and descriptively, is a theoretical and empirical question that will be also examined in the following pages.

In conclusion, this book moves deductively (though never perfectly) from general theory (conflict, situational, and small group) to methods of conflict resolution, and then to a particular form of such resolution, the *TMT,* and finally to the subsequent application of game theory to reveal the skeletal structure of those situational encounters where "decisions interact."

Recently, the U.S. Congress has held hearings to institute a National Academy dealing with Peace and Conflict Resolution. Such an academy will promote research and teaching in this vitally important area of learning. Aside from this proposed academy, there are other developments probably more influential—the most important being the several negotiation projects, now really an *institute,* on conflict resolution, founded by such people as Roger Fisher, William Ury, Jeffrey Rubin, Bruce Patton, Larry Susskind, Howard Raiffa, and several others at the Harvard Law School and Harvard Business School.

Negotiation and mediation are practically a cottage industry today with local mediators and consultants springing up everywhere from real estate to environmental issues. People are beginning to talk to each other first and mediation can work. It has made conflicts less frightening, less damaging, less costly, and more quickly resolved than other courses of action.

Conflict has come a long way since I first wrote about it more than eighteen years ago at Northwestern University for my Master's thesis. In fact this book is actually a continuation and enlargement of my Master's thesis stretching back to 1969. We hope it will prove useful to student, scholar, lawyer, consultant, and practitioner alike.

References

Coser, Lewis, *Continuities in the Study of Social Conflict,* New York: The Free Press, 1967.

Oberschall, Anthony, "Theories of Social Conflict," *Annual Review of Sociology,* Volume 4, 1978, pp. 291–315.

Jack Nusan Porter
Newton Highlands, Mass, USA

When Jack requested that I contribute to his forthcoming publication and after I had read his manuscript, I was impressed by the need for such a book. Many textbooks concerning this subject date from the fifties and sixties. Few books offer university students a combination of classical sociological conflict theory with small group research and international relations, providing a micro-structural foundation for the study and understanding of macro-sociological conflict analysis. In an increasingly complex world in which advances in information technology can either rapidly facilitate escalating community, national, and international conflicts *or* ameliorate them, all serious contributions to conflict resolution theory require discussion. I hope that I have made a modest contribution to this effort by providing a chapter reviewing the most recent conflict resolution theories.

Ruth Taplin
London, England

I. Conflict Theory: Classical and Contemporary

A. THE NATURE OF MAN AND WOMAN
B. THE NATURE OF CONFLICT
C. THE FUNCTIONS OF CONFLICT

A. *The Nature of Man and Woman*

Conflict theories arose as a counterperspective to the dominant functionalist school of sociology. Functionalist theory had been criticized for many reasons because it was essentially conservative and "utopian"; its approach was teleological; it lacked a focus when describing for whom or what something was functional; and the concept of equilibrium lacked proper definition. The most serious criticism of functionalist thought, however, was that it neglected the role of conflict. Yet conflict has been in evidence prior to the emergence of conflict theorists or even before theories themselves existed. The major task of our inquiry, therefore, is to first make explicit that which sociologists implicitly assume—the nature of man and woman—and to test whether or if these assumptions are congruent with either a structural-functional or conflict model of society.

Probably the most popular view of man is what Dennis Wrong has called the "over-socialized conception of man,"[1] the image of social man, of man the status-seeker.* Man is seen in his "origi-

---

*For purpose of simplicity, one term, "man", "he," or "him", will be used to refer to both genders.

nal nature" in neutral terms, not quite a "tabula rasa," but flexible enough to absorb all manner of content. Through the process of socialization, not only is culture transmitted, but attributes unique to human beings are acquired by man. Furthermore man is locked into a network of social relationships and dependent on others for support and cooperation. Wrong criticizes this view for not analyzing sufficiently those aspects of man that remain unsocialized. He refers to a Freudian concept which proposes that man's very social nature is the source of conflict and antagonism and creates resistance to complete socialization.

This perspective, often called the Hobbesian perspective of man, has been delineated by others such as Machiavelli, Hume, and Kant who view man as driven by self-centered social forces—to secure wealth, power, and prestige. This perspective is in direct opposition to one that can be traced to an image of man held by the Enlightenment philosophers—such as Locke, Montesquieu, John Stuart Mill, and Rousseau—It is a view congruent with a structural-functionalist model of society that sees man as goal-seeking, satus-seeking, and boundary-maintaining. As is often the case we may have to seek a middle path between these models. Inkeles argued in relation to this debate:

> While holding that man's antisocial and self-centered impulses can either be restrained or channeled to serve the public good, they (sociologists) acknowledge that in the process man must inevitably suffer some important restraints on the free and untrammeled expression of his impulses. Despite these restraints, sociologists argue, on balance, social life leaves man infinitely more free for development and self-expression that he could be in any unconceivable unsocialized state of nature.[2]

There is no "correct" image of man. We see that as long as there is a scarcity of freedoms, statuses and resources for the dispersal of man, there will be competition and conflict over the rights to such resource. Furthermore, particular men are more competent, more powerful, and more prestigious than others; and their valued positions are opposed by those without such power and prestige. Therefore, inequality was a natural consequence of the allocation of scarce goods and differential rewards, leading to such phenomena as stratificational systems and social conflict. If this "Marxist" position explains conflict, so too does a "Freudian" interpretation which views man as a social animal who is never completely socialized—because his idiosyncratic psychological variables also lead to conflictual behavior. On the micro and well as the macro level, conflict is apparent as no social system is conflict-free. Just as we can understand that conflict exists between macro-structures such as nation-states, classes, and complex organizations so too conflict exists within micro-structures, such as between the dyad and triad. In this book we assume that the concept of conflict (as well as of conflict resolution) will be used fluidly and flexibly enough to apply it to many forms of interaction and to many levels of complexity.

B. The Nature of Conflict

Simmel has stated: "The sociological significance of conflict (*Kampf*) has in principle never been disputed. Conflict is admitted to cause or modify interest groups, unifications, organizations . . . (and) it itself is a form of sociation."[3] Conflict as a form of social interaction is important for our present discussion, for it makes possible the confluence of parties so that conflict may be resolved. Boulding has defined conflict as a "situation of competition in which parties are aware of the incompatibility of potentially future positions and in which each party wishes to occupy a position that is incompatible with the wishes of the other."[4] Conflict is viewed here as part of the broader concept of competition. Competition exists when any potential position of two behaviorial units (a person, family, species of animal, class of ideas, social organization, nation-state) are mutually incompatible. While all cases of conflict involve competition, not all cases of competition involve conflict. Conflict then is a concomitant of competition over scarce goods. These "goods" can be either real or imagined: they can be tangible or abstract resources such as freedom, pride, or status. Group and individual social experience tends to be conflictual because it is often a response to the reality of shortages of scarce and advantageous resources.

Simmel has also pointed out that there are two major facets to the concept of conflict: the objective and the subjective. The conflict may focus on purely objective criteria leaving out all personal elements or it may include subjective elements. Face-to-face confrontation presupposes subjective goal and objective result. In the realm of competition, it is best explained by a quote from Simmel:

> If one fights with somebody to obtain his money, wife, or
> fame, one uses quite other forms and techniques than if one
> *competes* with him as to who is to channel the publics'
> money into his pockets, who is to win a woman's favor,
> who, by deed or word, is to make a greater name for
> himself.[5]

In the former situation, the adversaries are known and their
goal is subjectively orientated. It is closest to a zero-sum game.
Object X can bestow its reward upon either party A or B, but not
to both entailing gain for one which is a loss for the other. In the
latter case, the adversaries are in competition but may not know
one another. More importantly, the objective *result* is the aim,
not the subjective elements of the adversary. The goal is objec-
tively oriented. These issues will be discussed later in relation to
conflict resolution.

C. The Functions of Conflict

Conflict has been analyzed by Simmel, Coser, Dahrendorf, and
Gluckman as having a positive, functional value for group structures. Simmel has noticed that "social phenomena appear in a
new light when seen from the angle of this sociologically positive
character of conflict."[6] Gluckman has demonstrated the importance of conflict within interpersonal feuds resulting from various
conflicting loyalties.[7] Coser has suggested that conflict within a
group can help establish or reestablish unity and cohesion where
it has been threatened. Coser perceived a beneficial and tolerant
use for social conflict. His major work, *The Functions of Social
Conflict*, was an elaboration of the suggestive work of Georg
Simmel and his "formal" sociology.[8] Dahrendorf, another propo-
nent of the conflict school, has succinctly stated: "Not the
presence, but the absence of conflict is surprising and abnormal,
and we have good reason to be suspicious if we find a society or
social organization that displays no evidence of conflict."[9]
What are the functions of conflict? A few of them, according to
Coser and Simmel, are to:

a) Establish unity and cohesion.
b) Produce stablizing and integrative elements.
c) Ascertain the relative strength of antagonistic interests
within the structure.

    d) Constitute mechanisms for maintenance and/or readjustment of power balance.

    e) Produce associations and coalitions.

    f) Help reduce social isolation and unite individuals.

    g) Maintain boundary lines between new associations/coalitions.

    h) Act as a "safety-valve" to reduce frustration and aggression.

    i) Produce situations for consensus.

These are among the basic "callings" of conflict, but conflict is not *the only* perspective that may be used to understand social phenomena. A multifaceted approach is required for a thorough understanding. The conflict model is as useful as the structural-functional model because social structures display tendencies toward conflict and consensus. Dahrendorf has reiterated: "We need for the explanation of sociological problems both the equilibrium and the conflict models of society: and it may well be that . . . society has two faces of equal reality: one of stability, harmony, and consensus, and one of change, conflict, and constraint."[10] These two models have been described by Dahrendorf in his classical analysis.[11]

Conflict Model	*Structural-Functional Model*
1. Every society is subjected at every moment to change; social change is ubiquitous.	1. Every society is a relatively persisting configuration of elements.
2. Every society experiences social conflict; social conflict is ubiquitous.	2. Every society is a well-integrated configuration of elements.
3. Every element in a society contributes to its change.	3. Every element in a society contributes to its functioning.
4. Every society rests on the constraint of its members.	4. Every society rests on the consensus of its members.

Both sides of this dichotomous scheme are meaningful and in a certain sense both valid and analytically fruitful in relation to societal evidence. They are presented here to describe the "Janus-face" nature of both society and sociologists. These are by no means "false" faces, but, in essence, two perspectives that emanate from the images of man that sociologists hold about the nature of society itself—a society that contains stability and change, integration and disintegration, conflict and conciliation, function and dysfunction, consensus and constraint—in other words, a model of cybernetic growth.

II. Situational Theory

William Isaac Thomas, one of the founders of American sociology, advanced the thesis that it is essential to understand the processes whereby actors define their situations. His famous adage is apposite here: "If men define situations as real, they are real in their consequences." This has become an axiom (though not always heeded) within sociological research. The manner by which people define their situation will have consequences for how they respond to the stimuli within that situation. Men respond to such stimuli in a selective manner and such selection is influenced by how they define their situation. This axiom has important theoretical and methodological ramifications. In sociology (as well as social psychology), extensive research has been done which has assumed this axiom in an implicit manner, but rarely has it been explicit.

The scientific observer must utilize what Weber called *verstehen* in order to penetrate the definitions of the situation prevailing in the group by the use of "emphatic understanding," the validation of hypotheses of any social phenomenon through the understanding of its "meaning." Subjective meaning of a social situation poses problems for the scientific observer. The "humanistic coefficient," as Florian Znaniecki calls it, distinguishes cultural (sociological) from natural (physical) data. In observing social phenomena, such as a policeman mediating a fight between a man and his wife, the social scientist has the burden of establishing these intersubjective reliability checks that are essential and necessary for proper verification. Furthermore, he must do so in the light of the fact that he is dealing with relatively short-lived, evanescent situational "encounters."[12] For here, not only do we have the question of empathy, *verstehen,* but the observation and description of situations in which *supposedly* there are few "ground rules," or ethics by which to play the game. We shall see that such rules do exist in reality.

Goffman, who was influenced by Charles Horton Cooley, George Herbert Mead, and Georg Simmel, developed perspectives about face-to-face interactions, communication of self to others, the ethics of "focused gatherings," and the rules as to how such games are played—all of which have important bearing on mediation by "neutral" third-party actors. Goffman weaves together three elements—individual, communication, and interaction[13]—to describe such phenomena as the *game* (a body of rules associated with a lore regarding good strategies) and the *play* (any particular instance of a given game being played from beginning to end). *Playing a game* is then defined as the process of move-taking through which sequential plays are made by the parties involved.[14] We will later link the situational definition of a particular form of "game-playing," mediation, to game theory. Another insight of Goffman in relation to defining the situation is as follows:

> . . . an individual's position, defining position as it tends to be used, is a matter of life chances—the likelihood of his undergoing certain fateful experiences, certain trials, tribulations, and triumphs. His position in some sphere of life is his 'situation' there, in the sense employed by existentialists: the image that he and others come to have of him; the pleasures and anxieties he is likely to experience; the contingencies he meets in face-to-face interaction with others.[15]

Thus within natural settings, these variables are part of the situational role actors utilize in order to effect communication and to seek involvement within the encounter. Goffman has provided a framework by which such communication may be transmitted; it is a framework which is altered and molded by the defined situation as well as by the responses of important others within the situation. "Face-to-face situations are in fact ideal projective fields that the participant cannot help but structure. . . ."[16] Goffman continues to point out that there is freedom to maneuver under the defining circumstances of the situation:

> Instead, then, of starting with the notion of a definition of the situation, we must start with the idea that a particular definition is in *charge of the situation,* and that as long as this control is not overtly threatened or blatantly rejected, much counter-activity will be possible.[17]

We will return to Goffman later when describing the structure and norms of the triadic mediation. In summary, let us reiterate that Goffman has reformulated and reinterpreted old perspectives that are relevant to the situational ethics involved in face-to-face interaction. He has pointed out that the study of such interaction in natural settings does *not* even have a proper and adequate name[18] and that the boundaries in the fields of "small behavior" are not yet clearly demarcated, although its existence remains largely unquestioned.

The following section will describe briefly the social-psychological aspects of a particular dimension of "sociation"—the triad and the question of communication and coalition formation within the triad. It must be remembered that this study is inherently selective, and thus only a *portion* of small group communication theory can be delineated; however within the discussion of the triad a more comprehensive review will be undertaken.

III. Small Groups: Theory and Methods

A. THE DYAD AND THE TRIAD
B. COMMUNICATION AND INTERACTION

Small group theory is a twentieth century phenomenon and the recent increase in research on the small human group has been noteworthy. Mills defines small groups in terms of "units composed of two or more persons who come into contact for a purpose and who consider the contact meaningful."[19] Such a broad perspective includes most of the four to five billion small groups on earth. There are also a considerable number of dyads (e.g., man and wife, two lovers, chess players, fortune teller and customer, and nearly all bargaining and sales interactions), and there are a smaller number of triads (e.g., man-wife-child, the eternal lovers' triangle, a mediator conciliating two parties, and the *tertius gaudens*). In the following two sections we will first describe the theoretical background to the structure of the triad and secondly describe the communication that occurs within it.

A. The Dyad and the Triad

The seminal work in this area is again Georg Simmel, in his authoritative discussion of the dyad and triad and the sociological significance of the "third." The dyad, the elemental unit of social interaction and sociation, has particular characteristics. Two of these, according to Simmel, are *triviality* and *intimacy*. Triviality

11

here "connotes a certain measure of frequency, of the conscious-ness that a content of life is repeated."[20] Intimacy is "based on what each of the two participants gives or shows only to the one other person and to nobody else."[21] The addition of one more party not only turns the dyad into a triad but changes the complexion and complexity of interaction. In addition, these twin ingredients, triviality and intimacy, are irrevocably lost or at least greatly diminished, when the dyad is expanded by one other individual. Here, coalitions and combinations increase (for the triad, a factorial 3, 3!=6 combinations are minimumly possible). Within the triad, each party can operate as an intermediary between the other two individuals. Important research on the triad has verified much of Simmel's valuable but incomplete analysis. For example, the work of Caplow,[22] Mills,[23] Strod-beck,[24] Torrance,[25] and Bales and Borgatta[26] has been noteworthy in this area. Caplow and Mills demonstrated the tendency of the triad to become a coalition of two against one. There has also been evidence of the fact that small differences in "power," "activity," and other characteristics of the members of the triad will influence the formation of the coalitions. Sawyer and Guetzkow have shown that the formation of coalitions among parties has relevance to bargaining interaction because it is basic to most resolutions of multiparty negotiation.[27] From Theodore Caplow, we can describe the basic assumptions underlying the six major types of triadic coalitions:[28]

Assumption 1: Members of a triad may differ in strength. A stronger member can control a weaker member and will seek to do so.

Assumption 2: Each member of the triad seeks control over the others. Control over two others is preferred to control over one another. Control over one another is preferred to control over none.

Assumption 3: Strength is additive. The strength of a coalition is equal to the sum of the strengths of its two members.

Assumption 4: The formation of coalitions takes place in an existing triadic situation, so that there is a precoalition condition in every triad. Any attempt by a stronger member to coerce a weaker member into joining a nonadvantageous coalition will provoke the formation of an advantageous coalition to oppose the coercion.

The six types of coalitions (adapted from Caplow)[29] are:

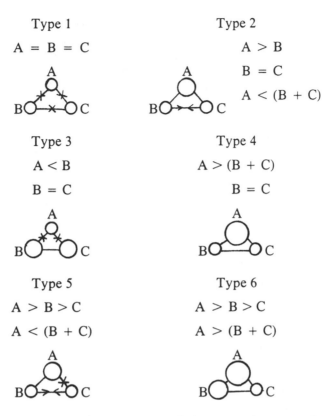

Type 1
A = B = C

Type 2
A > B
B = C
A < (B + C)

Type 3
A < B
B = C

Type 4
A > (B + C)
B = C

Type 5
A > B > C
A < (B + C)

Type 6
A > B > C
A > (B + C)

Type 1: In this, the simplest case, all three members are of equal strength. This is the classic but probably the least common type of triad.

Type 2: One member is stronger than the other two but not much stronger. Again, all three members seek a coalition since to be isolated is equivocally disadvantageous. However, the three possible coalitions are no longer of equal advantage.

Type 3: Here again, two members of the triad are equal in strength but in this case the third member is weaker. There are two probable coalitions, AB and AC.

Type 4: In this case, the strength of A exceeds the combined strength of B and C. B and C have no motive to enter a coalition with each other. Most likely no coalition will be formed unless either B or C can find some extraneous means of inducing A to join them.

Type 5: In this type, no two members of the triad are equal in strength, but the combined strength of any two members exceeds that of the third. This resembles Type 3 in that the weakest member of the triad has a definite advantage, being sure to be included in whatever coalition is formed.

Type 6: This is like the previous type in that the three members of the triad are unequal, but here A is stronger than B and C combined and has no motive to form a coalition. As in Type 4, true coalition is impossible.

In attempting to apply this scheme to various forms of mediation, we can see that an inherent goal of mediation is to form a coalition (a conciliation) between two parties. In terms of strength, the mediator is usually the "stronger" and seeks no coalition with either party. Therefore, it seems plausible that third-party mediation will utilize theoretically any type which makes coalition advantageous to each other and *not* take into account the possibility of coalition with the mediator. Thus, there may be initially little applicability to such theory to mediation. Yet, Caplow (as well as Mills) does add credibility to the hypothesis that the third party may serve to cement a coalition as much as threaten it.

Mills[30] attempted to answer three questions: Simmel's principle of segregation into a coalition of a *pair* and an *other;* the extent to which relationships are interdependent, whether the nature of one relationship determines to any degree the nature of the other relationships; and if interdependence develops into a rigidly set power structure. Mills' findings confirm Simmels' basic point that any threesome tends to break up into a pair and another party. Furthermore, *fear of the third party may account for the coalition formation.* Secondly, in the case of *tertius gaudens,* the situation in which conflict between two parties results in benefit to the third, there is found to be no general tendency.[31] However, as Mills states, "the principle of *tertius gaudens* can better be seen as an important dynamic aspect of the true coalition structure than as a principle underlying a type of structure all its own."[32] Lastly, the coalition is formed by the most active members while the least active is isolated. When this tendency is accentuated, there forms a genuine and rigidly set power structure with a stability of the pair demonstrated. In more permanent groups of three (father-mother-son as opposed to laboratory triads), Strodbeck found that no one person was singled out for exclusion in a series of decisions that might have led to coalitions. Finally, we might state that the switch in coalitions may have a tendency to maintain solidarity and avoid permanent exclusion of any one member. While a deadlock may be most severe and threatening to the stability of the dyad, the fluidity of the triad, the power of majority over minority, is quite conducive to the avoidance of deadlock and the emergence of conciliation. Though direct negotiations may be preferred (a dyad), the triad by its very nature may be considered a network that mitigates conflict through the fortuitous process of coalition formation.

B. Communication and Interaction

Communication and interaction are two concepts that have gained in stature since they were introduced to sociology by Park and Burgess.[33] In fact many of the social phenomena which have been labelled "interaction" may be more adequately studied as communicative acts. Communication in the context of the situationally-defined transaction is a complex process and is an important, if not the most important process, in mediation. It is the means by which the bargaining interchange is made; it is a method through which the use of threat, promise, and compromise are made and accepted. The interplay between parties is utilized to maintain mutual orientations and to facilitate inter-coordination through which consensus is developed, sustained, or broken. Communication may be defined in this context as gestures, verbal and nonverbal, and acts that are both transmitted and received. It is a two-way bridge. Goffman has defined communication as the "intentional use of a conventional set of symbols to convey something to somebody who is supposed to openly receive it; the message means the same to you as to him, and you tacitly avow and admit that it does."[34] Goffman describes four areas where communication has been utilized and in doing so ties together situational theory and game theory. (For more discussion on game theory, see Chapter VI.) These four areas are as follows:

(a) In the study of what Goffman calls "gatherings": cocktail parties, theater audiences, street traffic, etc. The essential feature is that the parties are engaged in a continuous face-to-face encounter. The central factor is not *essentially communication* (certainly not verbal communication), but rather the rules of conduct within a situational context. It is the code of unwritten ethics or proper behavior in the presence of others.

(b) In the study of interpersonal situationally based transactions to which game theory might be applied. Here the objective is to study the rights, obligations, and constraints upon the parties involved including all the richly endowed rituals that are utilized. This form of interaction leads us to a discussion of bargaining, negotiation, and compromise.[35] Communication represents the exchange of information, both substantive and normative which will enable an "equilibrium" to be established or reestablished. Equilibrium meaning consensus or similar forms of conflict resolution negotiated between the parties.

(c) Similar to the above area, communication is utilized in what Goffman calls "strategic interaction," situations wherein actors with either common or conflicting interests make decisions which are in response to the decisions of other actors. This focus centers on mixed-motive games or non-zero-sum games.[36] The emphasis is a departure from strictly competitive games (zero-sum) to those in which the interacters (interactants) utilize strategic opportunities in adapting to those exigencies of the situation.

(d) Finally, communication is utilized on a macro-scale through the use of mass-media, educational campaigns, and propaganda. In this case entire formal organizations are maintained to transmit and retrieve information. We will be most concerned with (b) and (c) of the above schema.

Communication may also be systemically analyzed through the analysis of networks, such as the wheel ◦⟍⟋◦, the circle, ◦△◦, or the chain ◦——◦——◦. We find that these three networks are the most common among triads. In our particular focus on the mediational triad, we see that all three networks are possible, but that the circle pattern is most likely to occur. Much work has been done on channels of communication: Bavelas,[37] Leavitt,[38] and Shaw,[39] among others. Leavitt found that satisfaction among participants was highest in the circle and chain patterns while speed and accuracy were higher in wheel patterns. Leavitt continues by generalizing that "the circle . . . is active, leaderless, unorganized, erratic, yet is enjoyed by its members. The wheel . . . is less active, has a distinct leader, is stably organized, is less erratic, and yet is unsatisfying to most of its members."[40]

Furthermore, the circle pattern takes longer to solve problems than the wheel. This is because a greater number of informational messages and reactions to those messages are transmitted among participants than in other networks. We may see that this information contributes to an understanding of nonexperimental triads in their natural settings: mediational transactions that occur in the offices of the lawyer, the marriage counselor, the labor negotiator. The circle pattern on the other hand is clearly an open communication network involving all parties concerned. Mediation, whether involving a family quarrel, a labor dispute, or an international crisis is best handled in a circle pattern (except, of course, where secrecy is necessary—then a wheel or even chain network may be more effective). Communication and interaction will be at a high level of information transmission but speed in decision-making will be less direct. (This pattern was reflected in the peace negotiations in Paris in relation to the Vietnam War.) The wheel pattern pertains to those triadic mediations in which there is no *direct* communication between two parties, and therefore all information is relayed and *filtered* through a third party. This third party may be considered to be a mediator, for example, conciliating a man and his wife. Let us compare the wheel network to the circle network:

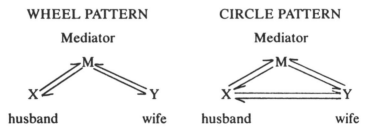

We may see that the chain pattern is actually a type of wheel network:

CHAIN PATTERN (TWO-WAY)

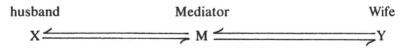

The wheel pattern will show certain characteristics contrary to those of the circle. There will be less open communication between parties and, consequently, less interaction. Less satisfaction will occur and more reliance upon the leader (mediator)

with a more stable pattern will emerge but it is a pattern that may be *less amenable to change and conciliation* than a circle pattern. Furthermore, certain mediational triads begin with the wheel (or chain) and then shift into a circle. It is possible to propose therefore that there is greater likelihood for consensus to be reached when such a shift occurs. The very movement itself, from wheel to circle, is an act of reconciliation that will bring a further measure of consensus to the parties involved.

IV. Means of Conflict Resolution

A. Avoidance
B. Conquest
C. Education and Contact
D. Spontaneous Remission
E. Transactional Resolution
  1. Direct Negotiations
  2. Mediation
F. Arbitration
G. Judicial Decision
H. Nonreconciliation
I. Summary

Conflict resolution is as old as conflict itself. If there has never been the "war of all against all," then there must have been a period of "peace." It is for those moments that students of conflict resolution wait. This chapter deals mainly with negotiated resolution-mediation, but other forms will also be described: avoidance, conquest, education, and spontaneous remission. This typology is a compilation and synthesis of many sources: the classical sociology of Georg Simmel; the conflict theory of Kenneth Boulding; research completed in relation to labor negotiations and international relations; and the vast literature of law and judicial decision.

Outside the arena of labor and international negotiations, there has been little work undertaken in regard to sociological mediation which is ad hoc, spontaneous mediation grounded in a situational context on one hand and institutionalized modes of conflict resolution such as marriage counseling on the other. For example, a compilation of bibliographic work by Meynaud and Schroder listed *ten* instances of sociological research studies concerning social mediation but over five hundred studies on the resolution of international conflicts (especially the role of the United Nations) and on the mediation and/or arbitration of labor disputes.[41] Such paucity of this type of sociological research was one factor in the author's initial interest in this area. Third-party intervention in a conflict, however, occurs in many fields and has given rise to a certain extent of a great deal of literature. On the other hand, even though there may be an abundance of material, it is a paradox that there is also a scarcity in one area. This has occurred because *third party intervention (mediation, negotiations, etc.) is seldom treated as a particular method independent of the subject to which it is applied.* The section on procedural conflict resolution will attempt to clarify and introduce some thoughts on this topic, but before we can explore this area, let us first examine a few of the classic means for terminating conflict: avoidance, conquest, and education. A fourth, spontaneous remission, is a new category, not usually introduced into this discussion because of methodological difficulties and is one that is original to this book.

A. Avoidance

One method for ending conflict, though usually not considered as such, is avoidance or what Simmel has described as the "disappearance" of one or both parties. Here, a distance is created between the parties involved. The term 'avoidance' is usually applied to the choice that individuals have when asked to choose between psychologically undesirable objects. The term has been taken from experimental psychology to denote the ending of conflict by eliminating *contact* between parties. This method inspires two interesting queries: (a) does this method end conflict in any *final* sense, or can it re-emerge in its former intensity in future interactions, and (b) does contact (and education) present alternative ways to resolve conflict? Thus we have two sides to the notion of *contact,* avoidance of contact and continuance of contact, both of which are designed to resolve conflict. Boulding has shown that avoidance may also be viewed in an economic sense to resolve conflict through competition. If a dispute concerning bargains occurs, one then seeks another bargainer. Avoidance thus emerges as a complex idea when scrutinized carefully.

B. Conquest

The most radical form of conflict termination is what Boulding terms "conquest" and Simmel calls "victory." Coser has also pointed out that when a victor deals the "death blow" to the vanquished, there exists the requirement of reciprocity[42] because the victor and the vanquished have made a contribution to the final "agreement." The act of announcing defeat by the vanquished is an autonomous act. As Simmel has stated, ". . . in this voluntary character of declaring oneself vanquished lies an ultimate proof of one's power. This last deed, at least, one can still do: one actually makes a gift to the victor."[43]

Conquest is usually thought to be an inimical mode of resolving conflict, and other means are thought to have a more aesthetic effect, especially mediational means of resolution. Yet, there should be no apriori value judgment placed on this method. It is a form of sociation, as Boulding declares, ". . . by which one of the parties is, in effect, removed to infinity, or removed from the scene, leaving the victor in sole possession of the field."[44]

Total conquest is usually an impossibility. A war in which the victor completely exterminates all members of the vanquished is a rare event indeed. In most cases, there always remains members of the vanquished to negotiate the peace settlement, whether this is done formally such as by peace treaties or informally such as through interfraternization between the vanquished and the victors. Thus when we compare avoidance and conquest, we may present the following examples:[45]

Avoidance	*Conquest*
Couples who do not get along, divorce.	Couples who do not get along, shoot at each other and one is killed.

Avoidance	*Conquest*
Customer who does not like a store, finds another one to shop at.	Customer who does not like a store, burns it down.
Nations that disagree, break off diplomatic ties.	Nations that disagree, declare war, and one exterminates the other.

The list could be extensive, but one may see that conquest is a fairly rare occurrence because of the immense amount of "toil and trouble" required to pursue it. Other methods have *less* of a zero-sum game outcome attached to them and require less energy. Of course, parties engaged in conquest rarely think about such matters or weigh their options in such a tolerant manner.

C. Education and Contact

Every introductory sociology and social-psychology textbook almost certainly contains a section on the reduction of intergroup conflict. Conquest and avoidance are however rarely mentioned while education and contact are very often emphasized in the literature. The context is usually one of interethnic or interracial conflict, and the methods of propagandistic, educational techniques or interactive contact will result in a reduction of conflict between the parties concerned. However, there is little mention of *root causes* or *structural defects* within a system that may not be affected at all by contact between conflicting parties or education of those parties. As has been mentioned, contact may have a "boomerang" effect. It may increase rather than reduce conflict; education may point out elements of difference and subordination that will only exacerbate existing tensions. (This may also be related to the idea of "revolution of rising expectations.")

The essential questions at this point are: what points are presented in the education? What is the purpose of the education? What are the discrepancies between the education and the existing state of affairs? Education which is usually a normative expression of communication is fraught with dilemmas. Because education has shown that it can be a tool in resolving conflict, it is regarded as a panacea for *all* ailments. We will not discuss to any great extent the role of education and contact. However, the very act of mediation presupposes the desire for contact, and thus the act of mediation is an educative act that *in itself* reduces intergroup conflict.

D. *Spontaneous Remission*

This fourth category is a relatively new one because of its somewhat "irrational" elements. Yet, if we are to heed the suggestion of Tiryakian, as sociologists we must delve into those areas of human behavior that are seemingly ambivalent and "irrational."[46] By spontaneous remission we refer to that form of conflict resolution which is seemingly without overt rationale. It is the immediate cessation of conflict and the movement away from further contact. It is similar to the spontaneous remission of physiological symptoms, usually of a pathological nature, found in disease states. Naturally a search will be instigated to find the underlying causes because both the doctor and the sociologist are "rational" creatures and will seek rational answers to a particular problem. However, just as there are questions that the doctor cannot answer leaving this hiatus open to the "art" of medicine to answer, so too are there queries that the sociologist cannot answer but does *he* have for himself a hiatus termed the "art of sociology"? To strict positivists, this suggestion is a travesty of the scientific endeavor but it is still a valid question to ask. The uses of spontaneous remission to reduce or end social conflict have yet to be analyzed in a systematic manner, but it is possible to present a few suggestions. The sudden unexpected termination of conflict may result from physiological reasons (the actors tire themselves out) which then leads to withdrawal from the field of conflict (avoidance). It may also result from nonverbal communication which states both parties agree spontaneously to terminate conflict with little or no loss of "face" or honor. There are other means by which conflict ends through spontaneous remission, but these two examples are adequate at this point in the discussion.

E. *Transactional Resolution*

We have previously discussed the methods of avoidance, conquest, education, contact, and spontaneous remission as means of conflict resolution. Now we may describe the areas that can be called *transactional resolution* of conflict. There is enough contact and interaction within this method to engage in a procedural encounter that will reduce or terminate conflict. Transactional resolution does not always lead to permanent termination of conflict, but it does facillitate temporary cessation so that more permanent conciliatory structures may be developed and maintained. It is important to note that the state of conflict may be a *component built into a system* (e.g. labor-management tensions) so that transactional resolution will be a legitimate but inherently temporary reduction in conflict. There exists four major subdivisions of this area which include direct negotiations, mediation, arbitration, and judicial decision. One final "method," nonreconciliation, will also be discussed.

1. Direct Negotiations

When two parties are able to settle their dispute without outside help, we have then a situation called *direct negotiation*. It is what Kahn-Freund calls an "autonomous form of settlement."[47] It is also dyadic and there is direct inter-individual communication unless subterfuge or silence is utilized to settle such disputes. A third party mediator is not necessary but when the need arises, the conflict level has increased to such an extent that the parties have moved away from the goal of conciliation. Mediation is then utilized and there is the possibility for conflict resolution to be resumed once more. The diagram for this method is as follows:

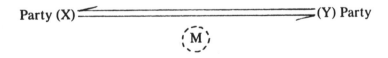

Party (X) ⇌——————————————⇌ (Y) Party
(M)

Here the third party is an unnecessary component but may be available at the voluntary request of the parties.

2. Mediation

When a third party is requested to *aid communication* but not to arbitrate (award), we have the method of *mediation*. (The important distinction between arbitration and mediation will be discussed in a future section.) Mediation between two parties has seldom been treated as a particular phenomenon *independent* of the subject to which it is applied. Mediation can be studied as a behavioral entity, as a distinct form of situational interaction with its own ground rules, pay-offs, rewards, protocol, and techniques of communication. One can, in fact, speak of a "norm of mediation" just as Alvin Gouldner speaks of a "norm of reciprocity." In the latter case, a moral norm is analyzed; in the former, a structural component, the mediational transaction, is present. In the next section, we will discuss in greater detail the structure of the triadic mediational transaction (TMT). However, a number of questions need to be addressed:

(1) Why do some forms of interaction *necessitate* a third party's intervention?
(2) What is the role of this third party?
(3) What are the risks and benefits involved in mediation?
(4) What is the protocol of the initial intervention by the mediator?
(5) How does a mediator resolve conflict? and
(6) What methods can be utilized to observe, measure, and verify such situationally based processes?

Some of these questions will be answered in this book while others will await further research. Mediation is far from a simple form of conflict resolution and it has its subareas which will be discussed below.

a) TYPES OF MEDIATIONS

Mediation may be conceptually and empirically broken down into four basic subgroups: initiation; inquiry/investigation; mediation, proper; and combinations of mediation and inquiry/investigation.

Initiation is the act of a neutral third party instigating interaction and communication by performing the role of "middleman," of a go-between, of a bridge over which two parties can begin to negotiate a transaction. It is basically a dyadic relationship, yet the third party is essential to the relationship[48] (for example, the role of the matchmaker is to initiate social encounters between a man and woman) for marriage purposes. Initiation is the simplest form of mediation. Included in this example is the use of "good offices"—whether they be used in international relations (e.g. the role that France played in utilizing Paris as a neutral area to discuss the war in Vietnam) or labor disputes where the offices of union mediator are utilized by the two parties to initiate direct negotiations.

Inquiry/investigation is basically a decision to instigate future communication by the use of "fact-finding" committees or individuals. This method is similar to the role that education plays in reducing conflict. It is a well-known method used in labor negotiations where the appointment of such a third party is usually made by the government, often with a view to mobilize public opinion toward a settlement. The committee of inquiry/investigation may or may not have the power to make recommendations or to arbitrate. Of course if it does, it then moves into another area of conflict resolution mentioned below. Kahn-Freud points out that the activities of the fact-finding board or commisison do not depend on the consent of the disputants.[49] Inquiry/investigation is a form of mediation that is quite useful but is often not the most successful (in terms of eventual conciliation) method of mediation. It is done without the consent of the two parties and therefore may prove inimical to them. However, it does prove useful when it is expedient to uncover underlying causes of conflict even in areas outside the particular jurisdiction of the committee.

Mediation proper is the method of conflict resolution that this study is most concerned with. Mediation implies third-party guidance so that any accommodation which is reached is mutually acceptable to two conflictual parties. In this case contrary to initiation and inquiry/investigation, the third party takes a more active role and is present during the communicational structure. It forms the essential third corner to the triangle.

Combinations of the above models are usually in the form of mediation combined with inquiry/investiagion. This may be a process by which an individual engages in a fact-finding investigation and later brings actual mediation into the proceedings between two parties. These four subdivisions of mediation have been briefly outlined, but further elaboration is necessary. The next section (on the TMT) will discuss mediation proper and also deal with the structural levels of mediation and their interactional complexity.

b) LEVELS OF MEDIATION

The following can be considered three general levels of mediation. The notation is simple: the X's represent the parties involved, M represents the mediator (or the middleman), the arrows represent the direction of communication, and the S represents a service rendered.

a) Mediation between parties who are on equal terms vis-a-vis status and/or power. There is little to no super- or subordination.

counselor

M

X₁ ←→ X₂

husband   wife

b) Mediation between parties who are on unequal terms vis-a-vis status and/or power. There is a definite level of super- or subordination. The mediator may respect such a level but may not allow it to influence his position and communication to the parties.

foreman

M

X₁ ←→ X₂

worker   management

c) Mediation between one party and another party who represents a *service* or object rather than a subjective interaction. The level of superordination usually rests with the service. The mediator assumes increased power differential for *initiation*, but does little in the actual mediation because the conflict level is low or non-existent.

pimp

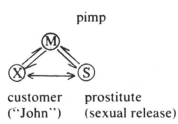

customer   prostitute
("John")   (sexual release)

This latter form of mediation moves into another area—which is one that may be called *middlemanship*. Here there is essentially an economic exchange, and the role of mediator (or let us call him the middleman) is to arrange economic transactions in the competitive bargaining and marketing structure. The relationship is basically dyadic (i.e., customer and seller), but as an occupational stratum, there are certain occupations which may be termed *occupational middleman*. For further discussion of this type of mediation involving economic middlemanship see the works of Porter,[50] Rinder,[51] and Stryker[52].

One final and important point requires clarification. Economic mediation or middlemanship is a *separate area* of analysis dealing with competition and distribution of goods or services. Mediation *per se* and its ramifications deal with conflict and its resolution. The strand connecting the two areas are that (a) competition is a form of institutionalized and "channeled" conflict, and (b) particular ethnic or racial groups have been characterized as economic middlemen (i.e. Jews, Greeks, Parsis). Because these groups have acted historically as economic middlemen, at times they have also been called upon to act as societal middlemen and have been asked to resolve interclass or interoccupational conflict—to be what may be called "super-mediators." In other words an entire class or ethnic group could play the role of mediator over and beyond its classical role as economic middlemen.[53] (See also the last chapter in this book.)

The levels of mediation (and middlemanship) may be arranged in a format based upon structural and interactionaly complexity. There are mediators on an interpersonal, interorganizational, interclass, and intersocietal basis. Two points must be noted at this point: (a) particular mediators (or middlemen) can perform at different levels, at different functions, and in slightly different roles; and (b) all forms of mediation are reducible eventually to an interpersonal basis. All that changes is that the parties then *represent* a more complex social structure. Such reduction is theoretically important when the mediational transaction of the triad is described in the next section. Thus, even when we discuss such "conglomerates" as nation-states and classes, we will continue to emphasize the fact that the parties are eventually selected to represent these phenomena and that a mediator must coordinate and conciliate these "conglomerates." Such levels of triads may be illustrated as follows:

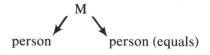

*Interpersonal
Basis*

Mediator(s)

person   person (equals)

host
lawyer
marriage counselor
matchmaker
policeman

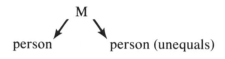

Mediator(s)

person   person (unequals)

foreman
lawyer

Mediator(s)

person   service

legitimate and illegitimate
    middlemen (brokers,
    pimps, etc.)

Interorganizational Basis

Mediator(s)

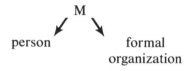

person   formal
                organization

ombudsman
lawyer
precinct captain
personnel office worker
guidance counselor

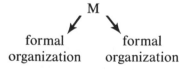

Mediator(s)

formal   formal
organization   organization

labor mediators and negoti-
    ators
lawyers
union stewards

Economic Middlemen

Mills' "new entrepreneur"[54]
    commercial research
    public relations
    advertising agencies
    labor relations
    mass communications
    entertainment industries

Interclass Basis[55]

Mediator(s)

class "ombudsman"
ethnic and racial commu-
 nity leaders and repre-
 sentatives

Economic Middlemen

"classical" or new entrepreneur
 money lenders
 pawn brokers
 mortgage bankers
 usurers

Economic Middlemen

commercial merchants
wholesale and retail merchants
salesmen

Intersocietal Basis

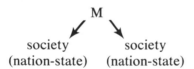

Mediator(s)

Ambassadors
Diplomatic couriers
United Nations (and its
 agencies and representa-
 tives)
A neutral country (e.g.
 Sweden, Switzerland)
International mediators
 and negotiators
Lawyers

c) ARBITRATION VS. MEDIATION

The essential criteria in the art of mediation is to (a) instigate communication between two parties where immediate contact is difficult or impossible, and (b) to accommodate those parties in reaching voluntarily and by mutual consent a mode of compromise and consensus acceptable to both. As Simmel has shown in his discussion of the triad, there are two (or more) dimensions of the triadic mediation. One, the nonpartisan, either produces the "concord of two colliding parties," whereby he will withdraw after creating direct contact (initiative), or functions as a mediator who balances, as it were, the contradictory claims against one another and eliminates what is incompatible.[56] This latter method has been called mediation.

The arbitrator, however, plays another role because he is involved in a decision in which he ends by taking a particular side. The mediator differs from the arbitrator in that the former *guides, initiates, and directs* the process of coming to terms, while the latter *adjudicates* the process. The mediator guides while the arbitrator judges but at times both are involved in the same role or they are confused by the parties involved (and by the general public). An example is the policeman "on the beat" who, while classified as a mediator, is also cast in the role of arbitrator. He can pass judgment as well as mediate, and these dichotomous roles cause his status to be both confused and vulnerable.

As Simmel notes succinctly:

> . . . as long as the third (party) properly operates as a mediator, the final termination of the conflict is exclusively in the hands of the *parties themselves*. But when they choose an arbitrator, they relinquish this final decision . . . he thus gains a special impressiveness and power over the antagonistic forces.[57]

Such arbitrational power is usually acknowledged by custom or law but the mediator does not have such power. His success is predicated on his own personal skills, not to any legitimized power to award. This difference between mediator and arbitrator is important to an understanding of the processes of mediation in general.

d) THE ROLE AND FUNCTION OF THE MEDIATOR

The mediator plays the central role in the TMT. He has many important functions in addition to bringing the two parties together by acting as a *catalyst* so that interaction and communication may be initiated. This function, called initiative, will not be discussed; rather we will discuss the role of mediator in mediation proper.

Mediators may be labeled either full-, part-time, or random. Full-time mediators are those whose occupational career is entirely devoted to mediation (e.g., marriage counselors, federal or state labor negotiators); Part-time mediators are those who devote only part of their occupationsl time to mediation (e.g., policemen, certain lawyers). Random mediators carry out mediation at desultory and ad hoc occasions (e.g., a host at a party, a person present at a quarrel in the street).

The mediator must possess particular social and intellectual skills that will enable him to bring consensus to a situation. A mediator first and foremost must be ethically neutral, nonpartisan, and objective. This commitment to objectivity implies not simply passivity and detachment but, as Simmel has stated ". . . a particular structure composed of distance and nearness, indifference and involvement."[58] The mediator must have a certain authority invested in him which will legitimate any suggestion that may influence conciliation. He must have knowledge of the rules, techniques, and conciliatory protocol that the situation requires. He must have particular social graces of sociability and flexibility so that extemporaneous adaptation can ensue to insure consensual stances. He must acquire those traits which will sustain mediation in interpersonal relations; he must be, as C. Wright Mills says, "honorable but sharp."

We may now describe a few of the functions of a mediator:

(a) To widen the agenda to include new bargaining variables;
(b) To introduce new opportunities to exchange intertransactional bargaining points;
(c) To put forward salient suggestions, making it impossible for the conflictual parties to lose face;
(d) To provide information to the parties on each side— bringing insights into the strengths, threats, promises, and bargaining boundaries of the parties;
(e) To help explore not only solutions that have occurred to the parties independently but to create new solutions around which a bargain can crystallize;
(f) To transmit messages so that accurate attitude and image change may be undertaken;
(g) To mobilize outside influence to bring coercive pressure upon the parties;
(h) To do all the above without raising the level of conflict and without antagonizing the parties.

With such a multitude of functions and multiplicity of skills needed to mediate, one can see the difficulty (and importance) of adopting the role as mediator in mediational situations.

F. ARBITRATION

There is little left to say about arbitration, or "award" as Kenneth Boulding has named it.[59] Suffice to say that arbitration entails less skill and conciliatory protocol than mediation since it relies less upon the skill of the mediator than upon the saliency of the award decision. Naturally in some cases such as labor disputes, arbitrators may also be mediators. Mediation is preferred in all cases to arbitration or judicial decision because mediation by definition implies *mutual consensus* which is favorable to both parties because of its independent and voluntaristic nature.

G. JUDICIAL DECISION

Judicial decision is a widespread and widely used form of conflict resolution. When both mediation and arbitration fail and if the situation is perceived as a serious threat to the state, judicial and legal intervention is introduced into the situation. Judicial decision places the weight of the law upon the discussants. Award (as in arbitration) is then made by a third party, which is in this case a judge or jury. The salient difference between arbitration and judicial decision (the "law") is that the latter has *more* coercive power behind it and is less open to preliminary mediation and conciliation. Similar to the reasons that mediation is superior to arbitration, arbitration is superior to judicial decision: Voluntary, noncoercive, and independent consensus is usually more utilitarian and satisfactory to the parties involved.

H. NONRECONCILIATION

This final category is similar to the first and brings us full circle from avoidance to nonreconciliation. In both cases, the parties have not resolved their conflict because they are no longer attempting communication which will eventuate in reconciliation.

However, in the first case there is no attempt at reconciliation, while in the second, reconciliation has failed and is spontaneously dropped and avoidance ensues. This last method is rare because societal sanctions will not allow nonreconciliatory conflicts just to "simply disappear independently," but will encourage the apparatus of the state, through mainly legal means, to pressure the parties to resolve their conflict. Nonreconciliation is a situation that is potentially explosive since conflict may reassert itself at any point in time.

I. Summary

Various methods of conflict resolution have been described in this chapter. They are not presented as an all-inclusive schema but as the major methods of conflict resolution. Emphasis has been placed on mediation and its ramifications with two major variables that affect all forms of conflict resolution. These may be labeled: (1) an index of coercive intervention; and (2) an index of voluntaristic interaction. The former describes the degree that an *outside force* enters the negotiations, changing the structure from essentially a dyadic to a triadic structure, bringing coercive pressure upon the parties to resolve the conflict. The scale is from high to low coersive pressure:

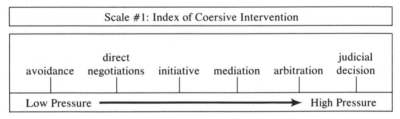

The index of voluntaristic interaction is an index of the degree that parties initially and voluntarily engage in an interaction that may eventuate in resolution. Again this scale ranges from high to low levels and is correlated to scale #1 in an inverse manner.

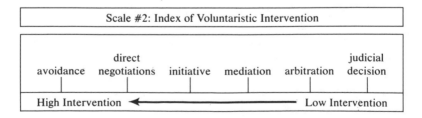

These are two scales, among others, that may be utilized in handling these multifarious methods. There is one final scale, which is the index of satisfaction. It shows the degree to which the final consensual resolution is acceptable and satisfactory to the involved parties. This method is biased however because satisfaction is viewed only from the point of view of the parties themselves, not from that of the third party, and more importantly, satisfaction is scaled from a high to low *imposed settlement*. Therefore high satisfaction correlates to low coersiveness (and low intervention) by an influential third party.

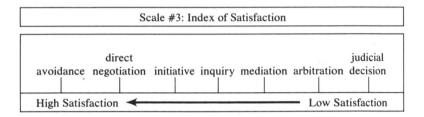

There is hope to elaborate and modify these scales in future research. The next section will deal with a particular form of mediation: the Triadic Mediational Transaction (TMT); a diagrammatic model will be utilized to illustrate the TMT method.

V. The TMT (Triadic Mediational Transaction): A Model

A model can be a useful analytical framework for the understanding of the behavior of a system, especially to the understanding of structural interconnections within a system—in this case the system of mediation, the TMT—the triadic mediational transaction. Models may be constructed in several ways. In the past they have been verbal, diagrammatic, or pictorial. Sociologists, until recently, have utilized the latter two to show, for example, the dynamics of social change or the flow of authority in organizational hierarchies. Recently, social scientists have translated verbal and diagrammatic models into mathematical models using a set of mathematical equations. For a discussion of the uses and applications of model construction see Simon,[60] Coleman,[61] Richardson,[62] Brodbeck,[63] and Beshers.[64] The usefulness of such models has been discussed by Daveson:

> When appropriate mathematical models can be constructed, the scientist has a powerful tool to aid him in understanding the behavior of the object or system he is investigating. The abstractness of the symbol system in a mathematical model makes possible the recognition of similarities and congruences between various models and thus between the realities they represent.[65]

A model may be defined as a physical or symbolic representation of a real or hypothesized system and can include any features of that system which are essential to the problem at hand. It can never include all the ramifications or all the variables associated with that system, but it may incorporate the essential features. Thus it is only an abstraction of reality. The system that this study is concerned with is that of the mediational transaction within the triad. The component parts may be shown diagrammatical as follows:

mediator

first party   second party

One example of mediation has been chosen as the basis for a model, which is an "ideal" or pure type: the voluntary mediation between two conflictual parties with channels of communication open to all. The triad has been broken down into a dyad (X and Y) and an isolate (M, the mediator). This follows the pattern discussed previously by Simmel, Caplow, and Mills, but, there are other features of this model. (See the chart on the TMT.) We have called it a transactional model because a basic element is the element of exchange, exchange of emotional and physical "objects" with the aid of a third-party mediator. This transaction is goal-oriented toward consensus, compromise, or catharsis to a degree satisfactory to the conflictual parties. The major components (based on the diagrammatic chart) are as follows.

1. *The Parties.* A transaction, as we have seen, involves at least two parties. These parties are, as Kenneth Boulding calls them, *behavior units* which refer to some individual, aggregate, or organization that is capable of assuming a number of different positions while retaining a common identity or boundary. These behavior units may be a person, a team, an organization, a bureaucracy, a nation-state, or even an inanimate object and are called *parties* when they are involved in a transaction. Transactions involve *at least* a pair as they may never exist in the singular. Furthermore, we may assume for the sake of the model that despite the complexity or abstraction of the behavior units, they continue to be represented and acknowledged as an individual (party X) involved in a conflict situation with another individual (party Y). Essentially, individuals will represent teams, organizations, nation-states, and inanimate objects (symbolic ideals) within the model—which also occurs in reality.

We will be interested in the socioeconomic, cultural, and personality backgrounds of the parties. The socioeconomic will include income, occupation, education, and style of life. The

The TMT Model

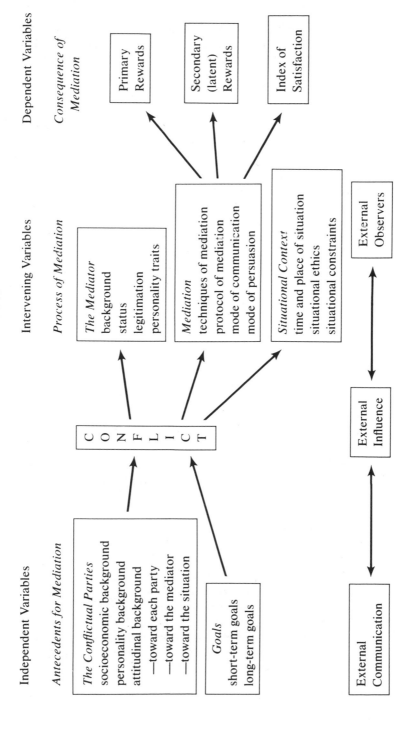

cultural will include the religious and political belief systems of the parties. The personality background will stress the attitudinal outlook of the parties in relation to themselves, the mediator, and the situation including those idiosyncratic dispositions that the parties bring with them to the situation.

2. *The Mediator.* We have assumed that certain transactions are not direct or immediate face-to-face negotiations and that the need for a mediator arises. The essential feature of mediation is its voluntary nature, and the mediator is voluntarily legitimated by both parties to aid the process of conciliation. Those traits of ethical neutrality or objectivity—trust, flexibility, sociability, and so forth—are essential to anyone playing the role of mediator. By the transmission of communication, in widening the agenda, neutralizing obstacles, and by providing cathartic outlets to both parties, the mediator is able to terminate or reduce conflict and to bring about some degree of consensus and compromise.

3. *The Goals of Mediation.* Both parties (and even the mediator) may come to the situation with particular goals; these goals may be specific or diffuse, long-term or short-term, difficult or easy to achieve. Some may be uncompromisable and may have to be abandoned. But in order to achieve satisfactory outcomes for the parties involved, goals must be selected, discussed, accepted, and then translated into action.

4. *The Mediation.* The techniques and protocol of mediation require observation. These may be as subtle as Goffman's description of cues and signs of demeanor or they may be fully formalized and ritualized as in some labor disputes. Usually, mediation follows no set rules except those set by the parties themselves; it is both extemporaneous and fluid. This may create methodological problems, but it in no way detracts from the situational context of the model. Lastly, mediation includes those modes of communication essential to the transmission of messages and those modes of persuasion that are correlated to the type and intensity of the conflictual demands and the legitimized power and status of the mediator.

5. *The Situational Context.* Situational theories were described at the beginning of this study. This was necessary because mediation is a situationally defined phenomenon—the time and place of the setting, the situational ethics of the participants, and the constraints imposed upon the situation by either internal or external influences are all important features.

6. *Rewards, Primary and Secondary.* As a consequence of mediation, there are certain pay-offs to the parties involved. These can be dichotomized into what may be called primary and secondary rewards. Primary rewards are those rewards that are fruits of *consensus* through compromise and bargaining. The primary reward is, first, termination and/or reduction of conflict and the subsequent resumption of peaceful, relatively conflict-free interaction. The secondary reward more closely resembles the latent functions of any social enterprise best delineated by Robert K. Merton.[66] For example, the ability to sustain future mediational situations can be a secondary reward to the primary reward of initial modification of conflict through such mediation.

7. *Index of Satisfaction.* The measure of satisfaction may be done in a before/after design of the "classical" type described by Stouffer.[67] This index of satisfaction is a concomitant to the degree that the rewards of mediation are accepted positively by the parties. The higher the degree of acceptance, the higher the index of satisfaction.

8. *External Influence.* By necessity a model must be considered a closed system with its component parts working in accordance to the demands of the model. Yet we know that such a model, or any model, does not operate in a vacuum. There are numerous external "pressures" or influences exerted upon the mediational transaction. These can, for example, be external observers who may (subtly) bias the negotiations or the weight of public opinion. There is the problem of communication with the external system. When we utilize the model, we will be fully cognizant of these structures and limitations. The model is to be utilized as a *tool.* The important point to emphasize here is that the component parts of the model will operate in a manner that is comparable to a real internal system and will modify and adapt to those external influences that are present.

9. *The Conflict.* The key elements to the model are: that conflict is present; that this conflict is perceived by the participants as a phenomenon which should be terminated and diminished; and that third-party mediation is a necessary component of such conflictual termination. Conflict may be defined as a "situation of competition in which the parties are aware of the incompatibility of potential future positions and in which each party wishes to occupy a position that is incompatible with the wishes of the other."[68] This incompatibility is a major component of

conflict. Such conflict may concern highly desirable goods, services, or symbols, mutual or reciprocal needs, or emotional and social demands.

10. The Transaction Itself. The final "component" is the entire transaction in and of itself. Such a transactional model has a dynamic essence—we see that the model is one of cybernation—adaptation and modification of initial goals and dispositions to a position of compromise and eventual consensus. Each of the above named components plays a part in such consensus. These transactions, whether they are on the level of international politics (such as the United Nations) or interpersonal conciliation (such as by a policeman, marriage counselor, or clergyman), may all be based upon the TMT model of mediation.

Conclusions: Some Hypotheses to Test

The following are some hypotheses to test regarding conflict and mediation which may form a tentative theory of mediation.

Hyp. 1: Conflict occurs when there are at least two parties with incompatible viewpoints and each wishes to defend its viewpoint and displace the other's.

Hyp. 2: Protest arises when there is strongly felt dissatisfaction with existing programs, policies, and/or structure and when those who protest feel that they are entitled to exercise weight in the decision-making process.

Hyp. 3: Protest is likely to be successful if: the object of protest is clear, there are not too many different objects of protest, the methods of protest are compatible with the goal, the public to which it is addressed is educated and crystalized into action favorable to the protest, and if counterprotest actions are ineffectual. If any one of these is unclear, unstated, or inconsistent, then protest may fail.

Hyp. 4: If protest occurs over a specific issue(s), then there are three alternatives for those at whom the protest is directed (or its "allies"): (a) to begin talks that will bring about compromise, (b) to do nothing, therefore legitimating the status-quo, or (c) to bring in repressive measures to "end the game," and also legitimate the status quo. (The difficulties are that combinations of the above are used in practice and, that one alternative may be used on one issue and another used on another issue.)

Hyp. 5:   If (b) or (c) of the above is chosen, there is really no *resolution to the conflict*. Further protest is almost certain and, in case (b), further protest is completely predicted.

Hyp. 6:   If case (a), however, is chosen, that is negotiation and mediation, then the conflict is on the way to resolution. If other methods are used, the possibilities for conflict resolution are unlikely.

Hyp. 7:   Mediation is successful if both parties agree *voluntarily* to mediate.

hyp. 8:   Mediation is successful if both parties put trust and faith in the mediator. ("Success" is defined as at least temporary dissolution of conflict and a return to equilibrium.)

Hyp. 9:   Agreement is more likely to occur if (a) both sides are organized, (b) both approach negotiations with a capacity to mobilize coersive pressures, (c) both are willing to save "face" and are able to do so after transactional pay-offs are met.

Hyp. 10.   The mediator is likely to be successful if the following functions are performed:
(a) If he interprets positions and problems of each to the other.
(b) If he conveys understandings of power relationships from one to the other.
(c) If he facilitates the mechanics of "trade-offs" or transactions.
(d) If he develops alternative solutions that are imaginative.
(e) If he establishes confidence of each in the other.
(f) If he assists one or both in internal organizational problems.
(g) If he helps either side to predict the consequences of action on their own organizations.

    (h) If he can mobilize external pressure on one or both sides to change positions.

    (i) If he can accept public responsibility for solutions so that respective leaders can protect their positions.

    (j) If he can arrange place, pace, as well as produce such items as explorations, trade-offs, commitment, sequence of issues and so forth.

Hyp. 11: Mediation is more effective if the following characteristics of mediators are met:

    (a) He establishes rapport with both sides because he is perceived as understanding the perspectives, problems, and organizational characteristics of each.

    (b) Each side believes that he understands the significance they attach to the issues about which they are negotiating.

    (c) He is perceived by both sides as committed to the desirability of successful negotiations including their joint involvement in relevant decisions.

    (d) Each side is convinced of his honesty.

    (e) Each side is sure he will respect confidence.

    (f) He understands both the complexity and the sublety of the negotiating process.

    (g) He is imaginative and creative.

    (h) He is viewed as having social prestige with the larger groupings to which each side relates.

VI. Game Theory: A Probe

Game theory made a marked impression on scientific research when the classic work of Von Neumann and Morgenstern appeared.[69] Today, it is not merely a heuristic device but an important procedure in the technical repetoire social scientist. In fact, according to Luce and Raiffa, "game theory is one of the first examples of an elaborate mathematical development centered solely in the social sciences".[70] Great significance was attached to the future of game theory, but its importance as technique in the social sciences never met its high expectations. Rapoport comments:

> . . . game theory was hailed as one of the most outstanding scientific achievements of our century. Since those who are able to fathom the full significance of game theory are likely to also have an understanding in depth of mathematical physics, such evaluation can be interpreted as placing game theory in the same class with, say, the theory of relativity which also belongs to our century.[71]

Game theory has not become the panacea people had hoped for nor has there been as extensive an *application* of game theory in the social sciences as had been predicted, yet a game theoretical perspective has been found useful in quite diverse areas of social analysis: Norton Long described the ecological structure of an urban community as a series of interdependent games;[72] Albert K. Cohen defined social disorganization as a situationally disrupted or unviable game;[73] Thibaut and Kelley have presented propositions in a set of outcome matrixes that have shed light on such social psychological problems as interdependence, power and control, social norms, and status evaluations;[74] George Homans has shown how the theory of games has provided insights into the element of rationality as applied to human exchange;[75]

and Thomas Schelling in a classic book *The Strategy of Conflict* has utilized game theory to delineate (among other topics) international political and military strategy and bargaining.[76] All of these contributions depended on a working knowledge of games, gaming, and game theory.

What is game theory? Schelling has defined game theory as a concern with situationally based games of strategy in contrast to games of skill or games of chance. The action of each participant in a theoretical game situation is based on the strategies open to him, his choice among several alternative courses of action, and the subsequent actions of other parties. Decisions of strategy are made with the knowledge that they will either be in conflict or consensus with the strategy of a competing set of decisions. The goal, based on the minimax theorem, is to utilize strategies which will minimize one's maximum expected loss. We have discussed the game earlier in connection with Goffman. Let us now define the game as simply "the totality of the rules which describe it, (and) every particular instance at which the game is played, in a particular way, from begining to end, is a play".[77] A *move* is an alternative choice made by a player or by a neutral device subject to change, which is governed by the *rules* of the game. A game consists of a sequence of moves made by the players. The strategy used in a game is defined as the general principle governing choices, and subsequently, moves which will lead to a favorable position and will bring positive rewards to the player will be utilized. Strategies, in most cases, are defined before the game begins. There may be several (or an infinite) number of strategies. These depend upon the number of possible moves and the number of choices for each move. If the latter two elements are finite, then the number of strategies are finite. Strategy informs a player as to "what he is to do in every possible situation in which he may find himself while playing the game."[78] Rules govern not only the ways and means of making moves but also the mode of strategy utilized. When the rules are not obeyed or when no rules exist, tension enters the game and ceases to be the game that is described by the original set of rules. Either new rules are established or the game is abolished and disorganization ensues.

There are numerous types of games, and in fact one purpose of game theory is to isolate and define particular games. The types of games may be described as follows:[79]

    (a) *Real vs. Non-real games*. Real games have a referent in the "real" world while non-real games have no such referrent. For example, a game involving Russia vs. America is a real game as compared to Alphaville vs. Betaville which is a non-real game.

(b) *Objective vs. Subjective games.* Games that are essentially abstractions or models as compared to "real-world" games. Most games used in game theory are abstractions drawn from a more complex game found in the "real world."

(c) *Competitive vs. Non-competitive games.* Games over which there is a conflict of interests and a mutually incompatible set of positions as compared to games that are merely "interaction," simply an interchange of goods, services, or communicative moves with no intent for competition to develop.

(d) *Zero-sum vs. Non-zero-sum games.* Games that are "pure" conflict (i.e., what X wins in terms of a defined set of rewards, Y loses) with the end result of the win-loss being zero, as opposed to games of "mixed-motive" (Schelling's term) where both players can end with a profit. The latter entails a modicum of cooperation and bargaining. The majority of games are non-zero-sum games.

(e) *Directed vs. Non-directed games.* Games in which players are under the jurisdiction of a director, umpire, or mediator as opposed to those games where there are no such mediators, arbitrators, or directors.

(f) *Perfect Information vs. Non-perfect information games.* Games, such as chess, in which with each move all players knows the position of the game as opposed to games, such as poker, in which no player knows with certainty the position of the game after each move. In the former, there is no probabilistic elements left to chance while in the latter chance is an important element of the game.

The list can continue, but we have described the major sets of games. However, what are the assumptions underlying game theory? We need to understand them because no game may be described theoretically unless these assumptions are fully understood:[80]

(a) "Rational" players are assumed. These are players who are consistent in their choice of risk-filled alternative moves and strategies, who will choose alternatives that will reward them with the maximum payoff allowable (or possible), and who will seek to minimize any losses. For example, the adult who on purpose loses to a child displays characteristics that are outside the realm of the game since "irrationality" is present when the decision to lose is made by the adult.

(b) There must be at least two players. No transaction can be undertaken with only one party.

(c) Situations must result as the outcome of sequential moves. The situation will determine who is to make the next move and what alternatives are available.

(d) Pay-offs must be specified on an interval scale. When they are, they are called *utilities*. We assume that a player maximizes his utilities and, furthermore, knows the preference patterns of the utilities of other players. Naturally, in reality it is difficult to know fully these patterns or to identify expected utilities with their corresponding strategy. For example, a player who bluffs for the thrill of bluffing is committing a strategy for which the proper utility (pay-off) function is ambiguous or undefined. These "irrational aspects" are explainable only on a psychological or social-psychological level and, as such, become elements outside the norms of game theory.

(e) There is a *termination rule,* which is a move that terminates play and ends the game. For example "checkmate" is the termination rule in chess. Each play of a game ends in a certain situation, and each situation determines a pay-off to each bona fide player. A bona fide player is defined as one who makes rational choices according to the rules of the game and receives pay-offs.

Now the question arises as to whether situations exist which include all the above qualities. Are players completely rational and aware of their utility functions? It is likely that they are not, and it is possible to ask, if game theory may be applied to social behavior, both normative and descriptive? The limitations of game theory will be discussed further on but it is possible to state that the essential transactions of game theory are isomorphic to the transactions played in the "outside" world. The difference (and it is important) is that game theory isolates the skeletal structure of interacting parties and therefore defines elemental forms on a high level of generalization by utilizing only *segments* of real-life situations.

Mediation in game theory is important to our present concerns. Game theory had been in the past "constrained" by the use of zero-sum games. Variable-sum games (non-zero-sum or mixed-motive games), however, utilize threats and promises, collaboration and accommodation, and it is within these games that the mediator (or arbitrator) is helpful. As has been shown the mediator can aid communication. However, in non-zero-sum games, communication is limited because it can only occur before the game begins in order to allow the players to agree as to how pay-offs are to be distributed. Yet, the mediator can make potent suggestions that will lead to consensus. Figure 1 shows a game matrix which can be mediated:

Figure 1

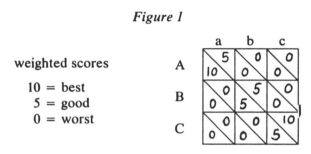

weighted scores

10 = best
5 = good
0 = worst

There seems to be no dominating strategy except that which the mediator can suggest to both parties to converge upon (B,b) as a consensual point of common interest. Here is a case of *pure mediation*. Figure 2 shows a situation where there is no point of equilibriation and therefore a third party acts as a *pure arbitrator* who must therefore choose between (A,a) and (B,b).

Figure 2

10 = best
5 = good
0 = worst

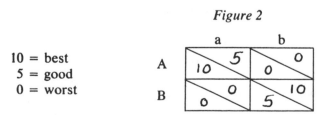

As Schelling points out:

> Mediators may be converted into arbitrators by the irrevoca-
> ble surrender of authority to him by the players. But arbitra-
> tion agreements have to be made enforcible by the players
> deliberately incurring jeopardy, providing the referee with
> the power to punish or surrendering to him something com-
> plementary to their own value systems . . .; two people who
> do not trust each other may find a third person that they both
> trust, and let him hold the stakes.[81]

Trust and the power to offer potent suggestions are essential to
the mediator when he undertakes negotiation. In both Figures 1
and 2, the mediator stands *outside* the outcome matrix and only
enters the situation at the request of the parties to either mediate
when conflict is at a low and compromising level, or to arbitrate
when the conflict level has risen, an impasse has been reached,
communication has become unviable for both parties, or mediated compromise unlikely.

Now let us present a concrete situation in which mediation
may be necessary once more. It is a situation that has immediate
significance today. Let us call it the student-administration game
(or *SAG,* for short). The "social arbiter," to use Luce and
Raiffa's term, here may be a neutral mediator or a mediation
board (a faculty committee, for example, if acceptable to both
sides). This mediation board will take into account the mutual
preferences and strategic potentialities of each party and aid in
the promotion of an equitable resolution to the conflict. *SAG* can,
of course, contain other potential parties aside from students and
administrators such as trustees, other faculty, police, but for our
purposes the administration will be represented by the dean of

Figure 3

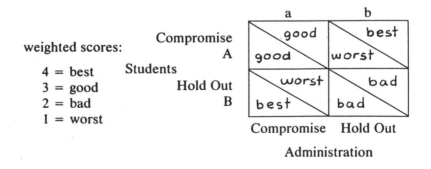

weighted scores:

4 = best
3 = good
2 = bad
1 = worst

students. "Students" is also a vague term since there are many groups of students, each with their particular perspectives and many with little "consciousness of kind." Among the many "power" groups on campus—such as political activists, right-wing fraternities, apathetic commuters, and so forth, we will use black (Afro-American) students to represent the "students." Finally we will assume that the criteria for game theory previously listed are understood to be presumptive (i.e., the rationality of each player).

Figure 4

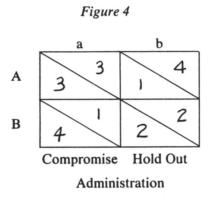

Compromise   Hold Out

Administration

Let us suppose that there has been a "take-over" of some administration offices by the Afro-American organization on campus and their demands include black history courses, a black student adviser, and a black student house. The alternatives open to the administration (and to the black students) are to either compromise, gain some concessions and not others, or "hold out," maintaining the status quo until the demands are met (or until the police come and terminate the game). The available utilities state that each party can compromise or hold out and that it is best for one party (and worst for the other party) to hold out while the other compromises, and that it is better for both parties to compromise than for both to hold out. This has been described by Sawyer and Rapoport-Chammah as the Prisoner's Dilemma.[82] The "classic" matrix for it is as follows:

Mediation may be used at the request of the conflicting parties, by directing both parties to that position where there is the greatest *joint* pay-off, and in Figure 3 it is (Good/Good); in Figure 4, it is the numerically weighted scores of (3,3), and in Figure 5, it is (Good for Both). This is naturally the "rational" approach and

Figure 5

Party B

		Compromise	Hold Out
	Compromise	Good for both	Worst for A Best for B
Party A			
	Hold Out	Best for A Worst for B	Bad for Both

the approach for which the *mediator can gain his greatest pay-off*, (e.g., the prestige of a mediator or satisfaction of a mediation board will increase when a compromise *good for both* is found.) The black students may utilize "irrational" strategy (in terms of game theory, not civil rights) and opt to hold out and not compromise. Then the administration can capitulate and compromise or it too can hold out, which is *worse for both* (See Figures 3, 4, 5). The administration may also call in police to rout the students; the black students can change tactics; or numerous other events can occur *not* governed by the rules of this particular game. Thus, new games are formed and new strategies formulated.

Let us now examine a few of the limitations of game theory. There are three major limitations:

(a) *Communication:* Game theory is essentially a model in which communication is not utilized generally. If we are referring to a particular move containing communicative information useful to the other party, then there is communication. But if we mean direct verbal or non-verbal communication *during* the game, then there is none. We have noted that some non-zero-sum games contain elements of communication but only *before* the game begins. Theoretically this is a limiting factor.

(b) *Applicability:* We have stated that an assumption of game theory is that it assumes players are "rational" in their strategies. However, the "real" world is not always "rational." It would appear that this poses problems for the game theoretical perspective because as a theory, it does not truly reflect the empirical world or take it into account. However, we may see that it does so further on.

(c) *Inadequacy:* We have seen that most games are non-negotiable, non-zero-sum games because they reflect the real-life conflicts of human phenomena. Game theory is clearly limited and inadequate in prescribing measures of rational decision in such games. Game theory is, however, adequate in zero-sum games, but as Rapoport maintains, ". . . its application is ultimately self-defeating. For if one side can find optimal strategies in zero-sum situations, so can the other. No one gains. . . ."[83]

These limitations are important but should not detract from the overall usefulness of game theory. First, it does give one insight into the *logic of strategic conflict*. Game theory's nonnormative aspects should also be stressed as it describes in a logical fashion the way the game is played, and if it is played according to the rules, *it can describe how people conduct themselves in a conflict situation,* not how they should conduct themselves. This view, however, has been criticized by Homans who feels that game theory is a normative theory.[84] Secondly, game theory is not a behavioral theory because it does not explain the psychological or sociological background of the actors. It simply describes the skeletal form of interaction, free from the complexities of such information. Therefore, it allows the scientist to dissect and isolate those rudimentary elements and strategies that are basic and important to a conflict situation. Furthermore, game theory is useful in generating insights that lead into *other* areas which might further explain the situation.

VII. Conclusion

By necessity this section will be brief since it is less of a conclusion and more of the beginning of field research to test the proposed TMT model. We hope that students and scholars will pursue such research. We have discussed conflict and conflict resolution and have focused on the triad of conflict party X, conflict party Y, and mediator M. This is the basic structure of the TMT, the triadic mediational transaction.

In our discussion of conflict, we are faced with a dilemma. If conflict is felt to be an integrating and unifying factor in group cohesion, then what of conflict resolution? What role does it play? Does it work in countervailing directions? We can answer this question with a resounding no. Conflict and conflict resolution work together in unison. The elements of the conflict are the seeds of its resolution. In certain cases, where conflict is "built into the system" (e.g., labor-management or tenant-landlord tensions), conflict resolution is likewise "built into the system." It is formalized and codified by certain structures that exist solely to resolve conflict (e.g., mediation/arbitration boards; housing courts, etc.).

These are cases where conflict resolution is predefined and institutionalized, but what of those adhoc extemporaneous examples of conflict resolution, (e.g., the policeman called on the scene to mediate a family quarrel or a race riot). Here there are no written, formalized rules of the game for it is defined by the situation. Thus, the research on situational theory, especially the work of Erving Goffman, was reviewed in this introduction and is extremely important for our understanding of conflict.

Small-group theory and research has elucidated "elemental forms" of human interaction under controlled laboratory conditions. Mediational triads have been, and continue to be, experimentally produced and studied. The work of Georg Simmel, over eighty years ago, continues to be provocative. This introduction, however, has utilized situations that encompass field methods and less structured observational methods, but the same triadic situations that occur in real life may be simulated in the laboratory and the classroom.

What about the TMT? The model described can be tested and verified for empirical accuracy. The present analysis, basically a simple model, may be enlarged and developed into a general theory of mediation. Just as there is a "norm of reciprocity" according to sociologist Alvin Gouldner, so too is there a "norm of mediational exchange."

Empirical research will begin to answer such questions as: How do men and women compromise? How do they reconcile? How does the mediator help or hinder the process? How does he help to reduce or terminate conflict? Is conflict terminable? Can we train better mediators? And how should we go about doing it?[85]

The real work begins now—to empirically resolve the questions posed above—to extend, clarify, and validate the theoretical model presented and to build a conceptually strong theory of conflict and conflict resolution. This book is a step in that process.

Notes

1. Dennis Wrong, "The Oversocialized Conception of Man," *American Sociological Review*, XXVI, 1961, pp. 183–192.
2. Alex Inkeles, *What is Sociology?: An Introduction to the Discipline and Profession*. Englewood Cliffs, N.J.: Prentice-Hall, 1964.
3. Georg Simmel, *Conflict and the Web of Group Affiliations*, (Translated by Kurt H. Wolff and Reinhard Bendix) New York: The Free Press, 1964, p. 13.
4. Kenneth Boulding, *Conflict and Defense: A General Theory*. New York; Harper and Row, 1962, pp. 4–6.
5. Georg Simmel, *op. cit.*, p. 57 (emphasis in the original).
6. Georg Simmel, *op. cit.*, p. 14.
7. Max Gluckman, "The Peace in the Feud," in Lewis Coser and Bernard Rosenberg, *Sociological Theory: A Book of Readings*. New York: McMillan Company, 1966, p. 203.
8. Lewis Coser, *The Functions of Social Conflict*, New York: The Free Press, 1956.
9. Ralf Dahrendorf, "Out of Utopia: Toward a Reorientation of Sociological Analysis," *American Journal of Sociology* LXIV, pp. 115–127.
10. Ralf Dahrendorf, *Ibid.*, p. 127.
11. Ralf Dahrendorf, "Toward a Theory of Social Conflict," *The Journal of Conflict Resolution*, II, 2, June 1958. Further elaboration of the above thesis can be found in Ralf Dahrendorf's *Class and Class Conflict in Industrial Society*, Stanford: Stanford University Press, 1959.
12. Erving Goffman, *Encounters*, Indianapolis, Indiana: The Bobbs-Merrill Company, Inc. 1961.
13. Here Goffman and I have drawn upon the work of Thomas C. Schelling, *The Strategy of Conflict*, Cambridge: Harvard University Press, 1960.
14. Goffman, *op. cit.*, p. 35.
15. *Ibid.*, p. 92.
16. *Ibid.*, p. 102.
17. Ibid., p. 133 (original emphasis).
18. Erving Goffman, *Interaction Ritual*, Garden City, New York: An-

chor Books, 1967, p. 1. See also his *The Presentation of Self in Everyday Life,* Garden City, New York: Anchor Books, 1959.

19. Theodore Mills, *The Sociology of Small Groups,* Englewood Cliffs, New Jersey: Prentice-Hall, Inc., 1967, p. 2.

20. Georg Simmel, *op. cit.,* p. 125.

21. Georg Simmel, *op. cit.,* p. 126.

22. Theodore A. Caplow, "A Theory of Coalitions in the Triad", *American Sociological Review,* 21, 1956, 489–493; and "Further Development of a Theory of Coalitions in the Triad, *American Journal of Sociology,* 64, 1959, 488–493.

23. Theodore M. Mills, "Power Relations in Three-Person Groups," *American Sociological Review,* 18, August, 1953, 351–357; and "The Coalition Pattern in Three Person Groups," *American Sociological Review,* 19, December, 1954, pp. 657–667. See also "Development Process in Three-Person Groups," *Human Relations,* 9, 1956, pp. 343–354.

24. Fred L. Strodbeck, "The Family as a Three-Person Group," *American Sociological Review,* 19, February 1954, pp. 23–29.

25. E. Paul Torrance, "Some Consequences of Power Differences on Decision Making in Permanent and Temporary Three-Man Groups," in A. Paul Hare, Edgar F. Borgotta, Robert F. Bales (editors), *Small Groups: Studies in Social Interaction,* New York: Alfred K. Knopf, 1955, pp. 396–413.

26. Robert F. Bales and Edgar F. Borgotta, "Size of Group as a Factor in the Interaction Profile," in A. Paul Hare, et al., *Small Groups: Studies in Social Interaction,* New York: Alfred K. Knopf, 1955, pp. 396–413.

27. Jack Sawyer and Harold Guetzkow, "Bargaining and Neogitations in International Relations," in Herbert C. Kelman (editor), *International Behavior: A Social-Psychological Analysis,* New York: Holt, Rinehart, and Winston, 1965, pp. 493–494.

28. Theodore A. Caplow, 1956, *op. cit.,* pp. 489–490.

29. Theodore A. Caplow, 1956, *op. cit.,* pp. 490–493. For a further development of these coalition types, see Caplow's *Two Against One: Coalitions in Triads,* Englewood, N.J.: Prentice-Hall, 1968.

30. Theodore M. Mills, 1953, *op. cit.,* p. 351.

31. For further description of the *tertius gaudens,* literally "the third who enjoys," see Georg Simmel, *The Sociology of Georg Simmel,* Kurt H. Wolff (translator and editor), New York: The Free Press, 1964, pp. 154–162.

32. Theodore M. Mills, 1953, *op. cit.,* p. 356.

33. Robert E. Park and Ernest W. Burgess, *The Introduction to the Science of Society,* Chicago: University of Chicago Press, 1921.

34. Erving Goffman, "Communication and Enforcement Systems," in Kathleen Archibald (editor), *Strategic Interaction and Conflict: Original Papers and Discussion,* Berkeley, Calif., International Security Problems, 1966, pp. 199–200.

35. See excellent bibliography in Jack Sawyer and Harold Guetzkow, *op. cit.*, pp. 514–520. ALso see Jack Sawyer, "Experiments in the Resolution of Interpersonal Conflict: Research Plan," Northwestern University, April, 1966, (mimeographed); Geoffrey Praeger and Jack Sawyer, "The Influence of Knowledge and Normative Information in a Dyadic Bargaining Game," Northwestern University, (mimeographed), 1966.

36. Kathleen Archibald (ed.), *op. cit.*, pp. V–VI.

37. Bavelas and his associates, under the influence of Kurt Lewin, have done rigorous social-psychological research in testing the effect of communication networks (*who* sends information to *whom*) on group efficiency and satisfaction. See Alex Bavelas, "Communication Patterns in Task-Oriented Groups," *Journal of Acoustical Society of America,* XX, 1950, pp. 725–730. For further discussion see A. Paul Hare, *Handbook of Small Group Research,* New York: The Free Press, 1962, pp. 272–290, especially pp. 274, 275, 279–285.

38. A follow-through study is Harold J. Leavitt, "Some Effects of Certain Communication Patterns on Group Performance," *Journal of Abnormal and Social Psychology,* XLVI, 1951, pp. 38–50.

39. Among other works by the author, see M. E. Shaw, "Some Effects of Problem Complexity Upon Problem Solution Efficiency in Different Communication Nets," *Journal of Experimental Psychology,* 48, 1954, pp. 211–217.

40. Harold J. Leavitt, *op. cit.*, p. 46.

41. For a comprehensive bibliography on mediation but weak in areas outside of labor and international affairs, see Jean Meynaud and Brigitte Schroeder, *La Mediation; Tendances de la Recherche et Bibliographie,* (1945–1959) Vol. II, Survey of Research in the Social Science, Amsterdam: North-Holland Publishing Company, 1961.

42. Lewis A. Coser, "The Termination of Conflict," *Journal of Conflict Resolution,* 5, December 1961, pp. 347–353.

43. Georg Simmel, op. cit., p. 114.

44. Kenneth Boulding, *op. cit.*, p. 309.

45. Based on *Ibid.*, pp. 308–309.

46. For a fuller description of this viewpoint see Edward A. Tiryakian, *Sociologism and Existentialism: Two Perspectives on the Individual and Society,* Englewood Cliffs, N.J.: Prentice-Hall, 1962.

47. O. Kahn-Freund, "Intergroup Conflicts and their Settlement," *The British Journal of Sociology,* 5, 3, September 1954, pp. 193–227.

48. Of course, when a third party is *not* necessary is an empirical question that is answered to some degree when the initial question of why a third party enters or is asked to enter is explored.

49. O. Kahn-Freund, *op. cit.*, p. 216.

50. The topic of economic middleman has been explored in Jack Nusan Porter, *The Urban Middleman: A Cross-Cultural Approach,* Sociology Dept., Evanston, Ill., Northwestern University, 1968, (mimeographed). For a theoretical foundation for mediation, see Jack

Nusan Porter, *Middlemanship: A Transactional Model,* Sociology Dept., Evanston, Ill.: Northwestern University, 1969, (mimeographed). See also his article in *Comparative Social Research,* Vol. 4, 1981.

51. Irwin Rinder, "Strangers in the Land: Social Relations in the Status Gap," *Social Problems,* 6, 1958–59, pp. 253–260.

52. Sheldon Stryker, "Social Structure and Prejudice," *Social Problems,* 6, 1959, pp. 340–354.

53. Of course, one can argue that economic middlemanship is a form of sociation and could also effect conflict resolution—if not resolve it then at least modify elements that could come under strain. In fact, economic behavior can be seen as a form of social interaction; stiff and formal though the role of customer-seller usually may be, it is still a social relationship. In fact, economic relations precede in many cases, other forms, especially more intimate social, familial, and friendship relations. In fact, one could propose that economic middlemanship is the *first* mode of communication that one group will have with another group, especially if one group considers the other *taboo.* In fact, economic sociation may be the *only form of sociation* allowable and available to the parties in some historical cases, i.e. Blacks in antebellum South.

54. For a full description of the new entrepreneur, see C. Wright Mills, *White Collar,* New York: Oxford University Press, 1959, pp. 91–100.

55. For further elaboration, see the works of Porter, Rinder, and Stryker, respectively, *op. cit.,* plus the extensive bibliography on economic middlemen, especially the "classical" types, in the selected readings section of this book.

56. Georg Simmel, 1964, b., *op. cit.,* pp. 145–153.

57. *Ibid.,* p. 151. (emphasis the author's).

58. *Ibid.,* pp. 145–169.

59. Kenneth Boulding, *op. cit.,* pp. 318–320.

60. Herbert Simon, *op. cit.*

61. James S. Coleman, 1964, *op. cit.,* and James S. Coleman, 1964, b, *op. cit.*

62. Lewis F. Richardson, *Statistics of Deadly Quarrels,* Chicago: Quadrangle, 1960, and Lewis F. Richardson, "The Statistics of Deadly Quarrels," in Alex Inkeles (Editor) *Reading on Modern Sociology,* Englewood Cliffs, N.J.: Prentice-Hall, 1966, pp. 275–285.

63. May Brodbeck, "Models, Meaning and Theories," In L. Gross (Editor), *Symposium on Sociological Theory,* Evanston, Ill. Row, Peterson, 1959, pp. 373–403.

64. J. M. Beshers, "Model and Theory Construction," *American Sociological Review,* XXII, 1957, pp. 32–38.

65. Richard E. Daveson, "Simulations in the Social Sciences," in Harold Guetzkow, 1962, *op. cit.,* pp. 1–15, especially p. 3.

66. See Robert K. Merton, *Social Theory and Social Structure* (revised and enlarged edition), New York: The Free Press, 1967, pp. 19–84.

67. Samuel Stouffer, "Observations on Study Design," in Scott McNall (Editor) *The Sociological Perspective: Introductory Readings,* Boston: Little, Brown, 1968, pp. 32–41. (Originally in the *American Journal of Sociology,* January 1950, pp. 335–361).

68. Kenneth Boulding, *op. cit.,* p. 5.

69. Though earlier works appeared in 1928 and 1937 by John Von Neumann, game theory lay dormant until the publication in 1944 of John Von Neumann and Oskar Morgenstern, *Theory of Games and Economic Behavior,* New York: John Wiley and Sons, 1964. The original papers were written primarily for mathematicians and only later did social scientists become involved with game theoretical perspectives.

70. R. Duncan Luce and Howard Raiffa, *Games and Decisions,* New York: John Wiley and Sons, 1957.

71. Anatol Rapoport, "Critiques of Game Theory," in Walter Buckley (editor), *Modern Systems Research for the Behavioral Scientists,* Chicago: Aldine Publishing Company, 1968, p. 474.

72. Norton Long, "The Local Community as an Ecology of Games," *American Journal of Sociology,* LXIV, November, 1958, pp. 251–261.,

73. Albert K. Cohen, "The Study of Social Disorganization and Deviant Behavior" in Robert K. Morton, Leonard Broom, and Leonard S. Cottrell, Jr. (editors) *Sociology Today: Problems and Prospects,* New York: Basic Books, 1959, pp. 475–479.

74. John W. Thibaut and Harold H. Kelley, *The Social Psychology of Groups,* New York: John Wiley and Sons, 1959.

75. George Homans, *Social Behavior: Its Elementary Forms,* New York: Harcourt, Brace, and World, 1961, pp. 79–82.

76. Thomas C. Schelling, *op. cit.,* especially pp. 1–20.

77. John Von Neumann and Oskar Morgenstern, *op. cit.,* p. 49.

78. Anatol Rapoport, *Two-Person Game Theory: The Essential Ideas,* Ann Arbor, Michigan: The University of Michigan Press, 1966, pp. 40–41.

79. The author wishes to thank Theresa Carr King of the University of Chicago for clarification in this area.

80. These assumptions have relied upon the discussion by Anatol Rapoport, *op. cit.,* pp. 18–21, 34.

81. Thomas C. Schelling, *op. cit.,* p. 145.

82. Jack Sawyer, April, 1966, *op. cit.,* pp. 4–5. Anatol Rapoport and Albert Chammah, *Prisoner's Dilemma,* Ann Arbor, Mich.: University of Michigan Press, 1965.

83. Anatol Repoport, 1966, *op. cit.,* pp. 204.

84. George Homans, 1964, *op. cit.* pp. 951–977, especially pp. 960–961.

85. The author is certainly aware of the ramifications of these questions; some are really not empirical but philosophical dilemmas. To paraphrase Scott Greer: "If you scratch a sociologist, you'll find a philosopher."

New Theoretical Approaches—Mediation and Negotiation: An Update

As Rubin (1983) has noted, human conflict is a growth industry especially within the context of American society of the eighties. This increase in conflict has been heightened rather than lessened by the subsequent growth in the law industry (Rifkin 1982) and has given rise to several new approaches to conflict resolution theory and practice. One new approach that is increasingly utilized by the average citizen as an alternative to litigation is mediation. Mediation may be defined as a process that involves discussion, clarification of the issues and compromise which is facilitated by a neutral, usually third party (Rifkin 1982:265). Another new approach to the resolution of conflict is that of negotiation or mediated negotiation. The former refers to communication between two or more parties that communicate for the purposes of influencing each other's decision (Fisher 1983:150), while the latter incorporates a neutral intervenor within the negotiations.

This chapter, constituting a theoretical and practical review for the most recent literature that has addressed the problems of conflict resolution will concentrate first on the more established process of mediation and then negotiation. Mediation as a method for the resolution of conflict differs from negotiation, although they are related as means to settle disputes between more than one party in usually an extra-legal, compromising manner.

Negotiation entails more than one party representing their own interests within the context of discussion and compromise in relation to the disputed issues. Disputants accept the fact that they are not involved in a zero-sum game and they must both (or all) give and take equitably to achieve a compromise settlement. Mediation on the other hand, involves a neutral or objective third party who aids the process of negotiation between disputants. The mediator is acceptable to all parties concerned and is asked to help the negotiations through concensus of the disputing parties without formal power or the legal right to impose sanctions. The goal of the mediator is to bring the conflicting parties to an agreement acceptable to all (Laue 1981).

To understand the current interest in mediation from which concepts of negotiation derive, it is essential to understand the historical growth of the new entrepreneurial middleman in America as well as current shifts away from state intervention to an even greater emphasis on the personal.

Theoretical Background and Perspectives

The idea of a "middleman" which has led to the occurence of the present day mediator in American society has been discussed in classical sociology but mainly with regard to economic and race relations. Weber's (1964:239) "pariah people", Georg Simmel's (1964:402–408) "the stranger"; Park's (1950:194–195) "permanent minority"; and Becker's (1956:137) "marginal trading peoples" all were steps in describing this phenomenon. Later, Irwin Rinder (1958–1959) and Sheldon Stryker (1959) expanded the concept to include such diverse, cross-cultural groups in the "status gap" as Jews, Parsis, Indians, Armenians, Greeks, Syrians and others who fulfill the role of marginal economic middleman. Porter (1981) further refined and examined this concept by comparing economic middlemen across cultures and throughout history.

The urban economic middleman as precursors to the new entrepreneurial middlemen such as "go-betweens", lawyers and mediators, were usually engaged in sales or service between either the primary producer and the manufacturer or the manufacturer and the final consumer. Historically, however, they have been viewed as interlopers or economic parasites and have held positions in the social structure that were both extremely functional and vulnerable to physical and social attack, from both the upper and "under" classes (See Blalock, 1967 and Bonacich, 1973).

Traditional middlemen have been small-goods dealers, pawnbrokers, money lenders and money changers, itinerant salesmen, shop-keepers and economic expediters ranging up and down the spectrum of size, prestige, and legitimacy.

However, as rapidly industrializing nation-states stabilize, as economic administration and organization improve, as large-scale industrial and business bureaucracies spread, and as levels of standard of living improve, the roles of certain "old" economic middlemen (such as pawnbrokers) diminish, while those of what C. Wright Mills (1959) calls the "new entrepreneurs" increase. Large-scale bureaucracies in particular spawn such middlemen who prosper as "fixers" and "go-betweens". These roles are often adopted today by lawyers who may be viewed as institutionalized middlemen. All middlemen seek to mediate or expediate goods and services between groups or individuals whose direct and immediate interaction is impossible, dangerous or illegal.

The following are some examples of middlemen.

    A. Economic middlemen
        1. Classical middlemen (the "Old" entrepreneurs)
        2. New Entrepreneurs (Lawyers, "fixers", expediters).
    B. Illicit middlemen
        1. Bookies
        2. Loan sharks
        3. Drug dealers
        4. Pimps
    C. Political middlemen
        1. Ombudsmen
        2. Officials with "pull" or "protektsia"
        3. "Paid-off" officials or corrupt bureaucrats
    D. Academic middlemen
        1. School counselors
        2. Teaching assistants
    E. Professional middlemen
        1. Lawyers
        2. Labor mediators
    F. Industrial middlemen
        1. Foremen
        2. Union officials
    G. Social middlemen
        1. Host at a party
        2. Social director at a resort or on ship

3. Matchmakers, marriage brokers
4. Family or couple counselors
5. Secretaries

Such diverse middlemen have diverse characteristics, but the following traits are crucial in understanding this role since they describe the unique role obligations that a middleman undertakes. It must be noted that while some middlemen roles are professionalized, many others can be played by anyone in an informal, non-professional situation (i.e. a matchmaker or party host). Characteristics of middlemen include:

A. *Vulnerability.* the precariousness of the middleman position exposes him/her to emotional, physical, and political attack. Being a mediator can arouse strong emotions from the parties being mediated if ill-feelings emerge in either party.

B. *Objectivity.* the middleman has a commitment to objectivity in order to carry out his/her task. This does not imply simply being passive or detached but as Simmel (1964:404) notes, the role implies "a particular structure composed of distance and nearness, indifference and involvement".

C. *Knowledgeability.* the middleman should possess the intellectual, emotional, and social skills which can be subsumed under such words as "contacts", "fix", "rapport" in order to undertake often sensitive negotiations. He/she must be what Mills (1959:91) calls "honorable but sharp". (See also Porter, 1981)

II. Legality and Legitimacy: Two Aspects of the Role

The middleman role is often in a state of flux. As society changes so do the "rules of the game". Certain middlemen roles may be illegal or illegitimate at one point in history and later become professionalized and thus legal. Legality pertains to whether the position has been formalized and whether there are rules of behavior, enforcement procedures, and punishment of violators. Legality usually refers to a systematized and codified practice. Legitimacy, on the other hand, pertains to the *perception* of the role, either positively or negatively. In other words, an occupation or role may be legal (such as a pawnbroker) yet may be held to be associated with criminal or illegal activities (such as loan sharking or "fences" for stolen property.) In certain communist countries, there are people known as *tolkachi,* expediters for large industrial concerns who work within the bureaucracy to facilitate the movement of goods. These middlemen are technically illegal in terms of the law of the state, but are perceived as legitimate by the Russian people because of their important role in commerce. Thus, they would be illegal but legitimate. (See Barrington Moore, 1954).

From the two dimensional aspects of legality and legitimacy, one can form a set of logically related ideal types of middlemen:

		Legal Position: Legal	Legal Position: Illegal
Perceived Image	Legitimate	legal and professional middlemen (lawyer, union mediator)	semi-legal middlemen (tolkachi)
	Illegitimate	semi-legitimate middlemen (pawnbroker)	illegal middlemen (pimps, bookies)

The above typology is useful in highlighting the middleman role. Middleman groups and middleman roles are usually vulnerable; thus, they have a large stake in legitimizing and legalizing their position in the society. The middleman, even when legal, is still apprehensive. The role is in flux because of the position itself or because of the place of the ethnic group filling that position. Part of this flux is because of apprehension that the role may disappear or that if illegal, criminal sanctions will be brought to bear upon the middleman. Thus, middlemen are constantly attempting to upgrade their image and when necessary to legalize their profession. Let us now examine more closely the four major types of middlemen.

A. Legitimate-Legal Middleman

When the middleman has been labeled as legitimate by the "public", and, has been institutionalized by law with a prescribed set of roles and an ideology of mediation he is termed a legal (or professional) middleman. The lawyer, the union negotiator, counselors, particular types of ombudsmen, and even medical doctors in some situations (for example, the general practioner as middle-man between patient and specialist or between patient and other social agencies) are all middlemen. The most salient features of this type of middleman is a code of ethics that have become ritualized and legitimized and an image that has become profes-sionalized.

B. Legitimate-Illegal Middleman

The middleman can be labeled as illegal by the authority of the state, yet be legitimate in the eyes of the public. Thus, he is legitimate in the sense that he represents a mode of mediation that is acceptable to the public. The term *quasi-legal* may be applied to this dichotomous split of legal position versus public accept-ance. As Barrington Moore (1954:62) points out the *tolkachi's* activities can be seen as both functional and dysfunctional for the economy as a whole:

> By interfering with the intricate system of priorities he performs a definite disservice to the regime. On the other hand, by scaring up supplies that may be useless where they are, but are badly needed by his employer, he performs a definite service for the economy. Possibly his positive con-tributions outweigh his disadvantages in the eyes of the authorities, who therefore continue to tolerate his existence.

C. Illegitimate-Legal Middleman

Here we have a situation similar to the semi-legal *tolkachi,* but the difference lies in the reversal of legality and legitimacy. Whereas the *tolkachi* are illegal in a technical sense but perceived as legitimate and useful by the public, there are a few examples of roles that are legal but perceived as illegitimate, that is, bordering on the criminal or deviant. For example, a semi-legitimate eco-nomic middle man, the pawnbroker, is governed by strict laws of the state but his image is tarnished because of perceived ties (perhaps wrongly) to criminal activities (i.e. fencing stolen goods, fronts for organized crime). Other examples of roles that are legal yet tarnished in public opinion are bailbondsmen and even used-car salesmen.

One point should be emphasized. Both the semi-legal and the semi-legitimate middleman are "unstable" in the sense that their positions can become legalized or "illegalized" by moving into a criminal or deviant career pattern. Since such middlemen straddle the thin line between deviance and conformity, they can move in either direction. Certainly, social legality can be attained as illustrated by the example of union officials or medical abortionists who can become acceptable as societal mores change; or the pawnbroker can become a jeweler and improve his image with a clean bright store and new merchandise. (The latter is similar to Ned Polsky's (1967) description of the transformation of the pool hall into a family billiard parlor.) Or the middleman may move in the opposite direction, away from respectability and legitimacy, and into a deviant or criminal career: the *tolkachi* can be arrested for entering into "black market" operations instead of staying within the boundaries of legitimiate industrial/commercial concerns; the "fixer" can get involved with taking bribes and be arrested; the pawnbroker can be involved in "washing" drug or gambling money or become involved in loan sharking.

Such mobility, the movement into either licit or illicit occupations is a crucial characteristic of middlemanship, exemplifying the vulnerable position that the middleman occupies. Moreover, it points out the societal dynamics that allow such interstitial positions to function. The middleman changes as society changes.

D. Illegitimate-Illegal Middlemen

The last category, the illegal middleman, consists of those middlemen whose image is perceived as illegitimate or deviant and whose role or position is deemed illegal by state authority. Here we have what Howard S. Becker (1963:20) calls the "pure deviant"—the pimp, the bookie, narcotics seller or loan shark. The illegal middleman is often engaged in crimes that would be handled by a vice squad, and whose ". . . crimes typically have no victim, or more precisely and neutrally, no citizen complainent" (Skolnick, 1967:116). The bookmaker, the pimp, or seller of narcotics as middlemen are not interested in the "trick" or the "victims" themselves so much as they are concerned with mediating a transaction. It becomes clear that illegal middlemen deal more with a *service* (i.e. supplying illegal goods) than with mediating between two people or groups in order to achieve concensus or equilibrium.

TYPES AND LEVELS OF MEDIATION

The mediator and mediation theory of today evolved from both the concepts of the Legitimate-Legal Middleman and the Legitimate-Illegal Middleman. It was a combination of public dissatisfaction with the legitimate lawyer and the growth of the "non-legal" counselor or community representative who offered counseling for local dispute settlement that led to a rise in the establishment of mediation services. Mediation evolved from this background at three different levels (X represents the parties involved in mediation, (M) represents the middleman/mediator, S represents a service rendered and the lines represent the direction of such mediation).

1) Mediation between parties who are on equal terms in relation to status or power. There is no super- or subordination: For example, two friends who are quarreling:

X_1 ---------------------------------(M)---------------------------------X_2

friend   counselor   friend

2) Mediation between parties who are unequal in terms of status and/or power. The status/power differential assumes different stresses upon the mediator. For example:

X---------------------------------(M)---------------------------------Y

worker   foreman   management

3) Mediation between one party and an inanimate object or service. There is no arbitration. The mediator assumes an increased power differential. For example:

X ---------------------------------(M) ---------------------------------S

gambler   bookie   the race, match, or game
drug user   drug dealer   the drug

Such levels of mediation can be utilized in a format based upon structural and interactional complexity. There are mediators on many levels: inter-personal, inter-institutional, inter-class, and inter-societal. One point that needs to be emphasized is that particular middlemen can perform at different levels, at different functions, and in slightly different roles. Thus, inter-correlation of role complexity increases the multi-variate forms of middle-manship. As societies and international relations become more sensitive, dangerous, and complex, there is need of more and more middlemen capable of the tasks confronting them. In short, professional middlemen mediators (diplomats, economic go-be-tweens, facilitators, etc.) are needed, some of them specially trained.

1) Interpersonal basis	*Mediator(s)*
	host at party
person ◄— (M) —► person (equals)	
	lawyer
person ◄— (M) —► person (unequals)	marriage counselor
person ◄— (M) —► service	matchmakers
	policemen
	foremen
	teaching assistants
	bookmaker
	pimp
	loan shark
	"fixer"

2) Intra- and Inter-Organizational Basis	*Mediator(s)*
	ombudsman
person ◄— (M) —► formal	lawyer
organizational	policeman
	precinct captain
	"paid off" official
	guidance counselor
	personal office worker
formal ◄— (M) —► formal	Mills' "new"
organization organization	entrepreneur
	commercial re-searchers
	public relations people
	advertising agencies
	labor relations specialists
	mass communication and entertainment industries personnel

3) Inter-class Basis

class   ← (M) → class

"classical" or "old" entrepreneur
money lenders
pawnbrokers
mortgage bankers
usurers
wholesale and re-
    tail commercial
    merchants and
    salesmen

4) Inter-societal Basis

society ← (M) → society
(nation-state)   (nation-state)

United Nations
A neutral country
    (Sweden, Switz-
    erland)
ambassadors
international ne-
    gotiators

THE RISE IN SOCIAL MEDIATION

American society and international relations have become so complex that a new role for middlemen/mediators has emerged in the non-economic but social role of reducing inter-personal and inter-societal conflict (see chart on page 71). The search for alternatives to legal institutions to arbitrate in disputes has been prompted by saturation with the multiplication of both laws and lawyers, accompanied by an increasing lack of understanding of the law, alienation, and the isolation of the individual in society. A problem with the law is that because it is designed to regulate observable behavior it focuses on the manifestations rather than addressing the causes of social malfunction.

The increasing complexities of the law within the context of modern society has contributed to the public at large sensing injustices while feeling unable to understand the origin or nature of the injustice. This applies in particular to non-professional and poorer people who do not have direct access to institutional resources. Furthermore, as Rifkin (1982:265) notes, competing sets of belief systems exist in American society, and judges decide which decision to make on the basis of prevailing norms, which to some extent may aggravate rather than lessen conflict as one party may continue to feel aggrieved.

Mediation which is compromised discussion between two disputants aided by a neutral third party whose judgment is re-
spected, has become a viable alternative to adversarial legal
processes in American society. It is becoming commonplace for
both civil and criminal disputes to be diverted from legal institutions to localized mediation projects of which there are over two
hundred in the United States.

Mediation has been viewed as a positive form of conflict
resolution because it is anti-bureaucratic and spontaneous, resolves conflicts through voluntary and consensual agreement,
and often resolves the underlying causes of the social tension. In
this process of compromise, mediation does not assume as does
the legal system that conflict is necessarily a negative, disruptive
phenomenon. The latter point has been used to support the
positive nature of mediation because conflict is more easily
resolved if it is viewed as a normal expression of personal growth
and social change. Mediation is perceived as a process that forces
people to reassess their positions and attitudes and to learn about
themselves.

However, despite the many beneficial attributes credited to
mediation, criticism has grown with the rise of its use. It has been
suggested that if equality in the judicial system has not been
achieved in the formal sector, it is doubtful whether mediation in
informal settings can compensate for inequitable power relations
between two parties. Power relations constitute a major problem
with the mediation process since the more powerful party has less
incentive to compromise or acknowledge the decisions of a
neutral third party that has no recourse to legal sanction. Parties
with unequal power bases would be likely to produce unequal
compromises and decisions, and it is possible that the mediator
may feel obliged to side with the powerful.

Finally, mediation in accordance with trends in the United
States towards personalization and a diminished role of the state
may be seen to encourage further privatization of life and exces-
sive concern with the personal. Such emphasis on the personal
often obscures structural conflicts between the state and citizens
or between classes which may also influence disputes between
parties (Rifkin 1982; Abel 1982). From an oppositional point of
view however, mediation may allow the state to intervene into the
personal lives of people without the legal safeguards provided by
state judicial institutions (Hofrichter 1982).

Mediation as part of the concept of middlemanship is subject to definition according to the needs of its societal context. Mediation is a growing but not a major social force as it remains peripheral to the primary institutions of society. Should it become a fully legitimate part of the legal institutions of society, mediation will no doubt change its character to some extent or serve to alter the nature of the institutions so that it will become a legitimate part of society. Mediation has already had another impact on society in the form of its related offspring, which is negotiation.

NEGOTIATION

Negotiation is a relatively recent phenomenon in terms of it being perceived as both a disciplined art and science that can be studied and researched. As Fisher and Ury (1981) note, all people negotiate on a daily basis whether it is in a legal context of a law case or in relation to a family dispute. Negotiation in its broadest sense is a means of communication oriented towards reaching agreement on the basis of shared interests. In the attempt to quantify negotiation and subject it to scientific analysis as Raiffa (1982) does, negotiation may be defined more precisely ". . . as the settlement of differences and the waging of conflict through verbal exchange. . . ." (Susskind and Rubin 1983:133).

Guidelines for negotiation as it has emerged from experimental studies have been drawn from a plethora of disputes ranging from labor-management to divorce to international disagreements. Negotiation as has been explained in relation to mediation was derived from dissatisfaction with traditional methods of dispute resolution and developed along with mediation as another alternative method of conflict resolution. Negotiation theory has developed from interpersonal analysis to international negotiation theory to negotiated intervention. We will provide a review of the various new approaches to negotiation in the following pages.

Positional bargaining is the model that most people associate with the concept of negotiation. It is the classical definition, one that is associated with bargaining at the bazaar. This form of negotiation can be effective and produce satisfactory results. Stock market trading is another example of how positional bargaining can be useful and efficient. In other cases positional bargaining can produce less than satisfactory results and describes only a small part of the possible types of negotiations that can occur between parties. Positional theories in traditional economics for example interpret all economic activity in terms of the desire of people to maximize their material rewards in life. Other economic theories which do not interpret economic activity from this perspective judge the economic goals of people in terms of maintenance of what they possess and not being "taken" by others.

POSITIONAL BARGAINING

Positional bargaining as a major form of negotiation has been criticized for hindering the development of other potentially useful options that could facilitate amicable agreement. The undue emphasis of this negotiating approach on positions and maximization of the bargaining position tends to produce intrangience, mistrust and bad feelings between the parties. The relationship between the parties degenerates and prevents open discussion of shared interests and inhibits creative invention of alternative options to the simple maximization of bargaining positions. This model does not take into account the fact that people may wish to establish good relationships through the process of negotiation or appear legitimate. In many cases such as banking or diplomacy in an international context, the relationship between the parties is of much greater importance than the substantive outcome in any particular negotiation as the negotiators have very long term goals. Positional bargaining on the other hand facilitates short-term goals because the parties focus on short-term substantive gain rather than a long term working relationship. Positional bargaining because it is often a contest of wills results in negative feelings such as anger, bitterness and resentment which obscures the issues and allows legitimate concerns to remain unaddressed. The strains of this type of bargaining may be so great that the bad feelings produced by such an encounter may last a lifetime (Fisher and Ury 1981).

Fisher and Ury (1981) also make the point that positional bargaining is an even less desirable form of negotiation in the event of multiple party involvement. Where complete consensus is necessary to make decisions in large governing bodies such as the United Nations, only one member need vote no to veto an issue. Reciprocal bilateral concessions are difficult to make and would not necessarily facilitate multilateral agreement. Positional bargaining would lead in this case to coalition formation whose constituents would not agree necessarily on all issues. Not only is it difficult to reach a common position through positional bargaining but also to amend or inject flexibility into the proceedings. Pursuing a soft bargaining positional approach has its problems as well because it is often likely that the other party is a hard bargainer and while the former is yielding to pressure to attempt to be accommodating, the latter will be applying pressure gaining all the concessions.

PRINCIPLED NEGOTIATION

The major new alternative theoretical model to positional bargaining is that of "principled negotiation" (Fisher and Ury 1981). Principled negotiation deals with recognizing the joint goals of the parties to come to an agreement without sacrificing either substantive gain or the relationship and with dealing with both these aspects of the negotiations on their merits. In the place of positions, threats or justifications, principled negotiators focus on principles, common interests, the multiplicity of available options and objective criteria which help to define merits, making them tangible to the parties.

The theory of principled negotiation proposes that if the parties involved argue about interests and objective criteria rather than positions, many positive benefits to dispute resolution will follow such as clearer communication, greater understanding, inventiveness, a better chance for reality testing of options and a much stronger relationship that avoids the need for face-saving. With the assumption being that the main concern of the parties is that they do not get "taken" the idea of fairness will be settled between the parties rather than having criteria of fairness imputed onto the negotiating parties from an extraneous source. For once people understand without hidden surprises the most salient aspects of the issues, it is fair to suppose that an amicable agreement can be reached within the limits of reasonable fairness that is agreeable to both parties (Patton 1985).

Principled negotiation as proposed by Fisher and Ury (1981) concentrates on the four following points that will be briefly explained below.

A major prescription in principled negotiation is to separate the people from the problem. Too often negotiations break down because the issues or the substance of the problem becomes obscured by personality clashes or problems of people's psychology. Understanding and agreement can become disrupted if problems with people occur in relation to perception, emotion and communication.

Perception involves understanding how the other party in the negotiations is thinking and how he or she perceives the issues under discussion. Understanding of this form is essential for the thinking of the other party is the problem.

Emotions, especially if the dispute is a bitter one, can breed anger and fear which may bring the negotiations to a quick end. It is important therefore to the continuity of the proceedings to make emotions on both sides explicit and to acknowledge them as a legitimate part of the negotiations. Allowing the other party to express their anger and grievances gives their emotional feelings legitimacy and makes it easier to deal with.

Communication is of the essence to the process of negotiation for without it no negotiation could exist. Communication, despite the fact that it is practiced by people all their lives is difficult to establish and maintain. People often converse but not to each other, either talking past the other person or for the purposes of impression rather than genuine communication. Communication fails as well when parties misinterpret what the other is stating or simply do not actively listen to the other person. Taking into account communication, perception and emotion therefore are a key to separating the people from the problem.

A related point which is necessary to help separate the people from the problem is to focus on the interests rather than the positions in a negotiation. Positions are what people have already decided upon, while interests are the desires and concerns of the parties that led to the positions. Positions tend to be oppositional and allow scope for finding common ground. Interests on the other hand are diversified and often a discussion of interests will reveal more than are shared and compatible than those that are in opposition. To concentrate on the interests vigorously, while showing fellow negotiators courtesy and respect will help to separate the people from the problem and not allow other parties to feel personally under attack which usually harms negotiated agreement.

Once the problem is separated from fellow negotiators and good communication has been established, it is important to use positive energies to invent options that are mutually acceptable for joint gain. Invention of options does not come readily but is one of the most useful skills for negotiators to master. Most people tend to rely on a single answer and view a conflict in black or white terms and are concerned to narrow options to move quickly towards their own position. Therefore to be inventive it is essential to create firstly numerous options without judging them so the critical process does not inhibit invention. Secondly, it's important to broaden the options available rather than narrow them seeking options that are mutually acceptable to both parties and presenting options that makes agreement for the other party as painless as possible.

Finally, when negotiating and creating options it is important to base options on objective criteria that deals with the merits of the problem, not the mettle of the parties. The negotiator should be open to reason but not to threats. When two parties battle for dominance the relationship becomes threatened, while principled negotiation protects the relationship, because objective criteria are discussed to settle a problem. Rather than parties spending their time either defending or attacking the other's position, time is used efficiently dealing with standards of efficiency, fairness and scientific merit to reach a wise agreement amicably. The more the parties refer to legal or common law precedent or simply community practice the more quickly the dispute can be settled with the benefit of past experience. Independent standards facilitate greater efficiency especially in the case of numerous parties.

To utilize objective criteria successfully, fair standards and procedures must be utilized, which are independent from each other's will and based on fair procedure such as taking turns, drawing lots or having another party independent from the proceedings decide on the fairest agreement. A third party may be involved in a number of ways as an expert, a mediator or an arbitrator. The most objective negotiations are based on a joint search for the fairest agreement which is based on mutually agreed standards. Standards and principles Fisher and Ury (1981) emphasize strongly are not based on the common understanding of principle meaning a commitment to a particular ideology as they believe this locks the negotiators into a further impasse. By principled they refer to criteria that are advanced by the parties at the beginning of negotiations which are mutually agreed upon. As different parties hold a variety of ideas regarding legitimate standards, an objective basis for deciding between them can be produced with both parties agreeing on their equal legitimacy. Through compromise and settling differences equitably on the basis of the merits of the issues can produce an amicable agreement. Principled negotiation is based on reasoned persuasion according to the merits of the issue.

CRITICISM OF PRINCIPLED NEGOTIATION

Principled negotiation as a theory has been criticized in several ways. One criticism is the lack of clarity of the theory. For example, although it is presented as a functional rather than ethical theory it does not clarify adequately how to balance legitimacy and efficacy in negotiations. It also does not provide clear rules for breaking lock in tactics. The theory regarding "wise" outcomes is never explained fully and the discrepancy between the results of joint gain trade offs and initial mutually agreed objective criteria is never clarified fully by Fisher and Ury. The overall relationship between talking and acting in unison with regard to the goals and principles of the theory remains unclear (Patton 1984).

Principled negotiation falls short in the attention it gives to issues of power differentials in relation to negotiation. As noted in the discussion of mediation the powerful party has far less reason to compromise and parties that have unequal power bases would be most likely to produce unequal decisions and outcomes. This problem of power has troubled the foundations of the principled negotiation theory.

THE ISSUE OF POWER AND PRINCIPLED NEGOTIATION

Fisher (1983) acknowledges the issue of power and how it can jeopardize jointly produced "wise" outcomes in the real world where amount of power influences results strongly. However, he maintains that understanding how important the role of power is to the negotiating process may be a truism but is an irrelevant one. Fisher believes that power differentials may be true in terms of descriptive analysis but has little significance for prescriptive action and action is emphasized in principled negotiation not scientific truths. Principled negotiation stresses how the power that a party possesses may be used to full effect and how to enhance that power. Fisher (1983) argues that power potential is cumulative and that people have categories of power potential that may be used in concert to improve their negotiating power.

These categories which will be outlined briefly below includes

the power of skill and knowledge, the power of good relationships, the power of good alternatives, the power of an elegant
solution, the power of legitimacy and commitment.

Both skill and knowledge provide a negotiator with greater
power because a skilled negotiator has greater potential to influence than an unskilled one. Skills which can be learned include
the ability to listen, to empathize, to communicate clearly to
analyze and to organize ideas. Knowledge is power as well
because the more information one gathers about the other party
and the issues to be discussed the more they can obtain power.
Basic knowledge of general negotiation procedures, styles and
cultural difference all facilitate negotiating power.

The better the relationship is between the negotiating parties,
in terms of trust and communication, the more powerful are the
negotiators because they rely on each other for mutual respect
and trust each other's commitments to carry out any agreed
promises. Building a good working relationship provides a powerful base for long term negotiation as in such circumstances the
relationship is often more important than the immediate goal of
obtaining a short-term result.

Having an alternative option that is not dependent on the party
that one is negotiating with provides a more powerful base for the
negotiator. Fisher and Ury (1981) speak of "BATNA" (Best
Alternative to a Negotiated Agreement). Making an arrangement
with a competitor for example, will force the other party to
compromise because they realize that if they do not offer something better they may lose the chance to negotiate. On the other
hand, the less attractive the BATNA of a party, the stronger is the
negotiating position of the other party, so the pressure exerted by
the BATNA can create power for either party depending on how
they use their BATNA.

Related to the BATNA is the idea of elegant solution which
refers to the power of creating a great number of options so that
the possibilities for meeting the legitimate interests of both parties are heightened. The more options a negotiator can create the
greater are his chances to influence a positive outcome.

Negotiators may also increase their power by adhering to
legitimate standards that are persuasive to the other party. Legitimate standards refer to that which is consistent with precedent,
the practice of industry or the law or agreed upon expert advice.

Fisher argues finally that the above five forms of power can be
enhanced by the approach to the negotiations whether they are

carried out affirmatively or negatively. The affirmative commitment aids the negotiations because it is an offer of something that one of the negotiating parties is willing to do. It holds persuasive power because it is an offer of positive action. Negative commitments on the other hand, weaken negotiating power because the earlier the negotiator announces a rigid ultimatum the less chance is the cumulative total of the different facets of negotiating power likely to have an effect.

All these points of Fisher provide ideas concerning the possibility of increasing negotiator power despite initial inequalities in power, but in practice a question still remains of whether fundamental differences in power can be talked away in negotiations. Other theorists have built on Fisher's ideas to improve negotiation strategies.

STRATEGIC CHOICE

Four basic strategies that are available to negotiators are located and assessed by Pruitt and Rubin (1986). These strategies include problem solving, contending, yielding, inaction and withdrawal. The first three of these strategies are viewed as coping ones because they attempt to move the process of negotiations towards agreement. The other two do little to further agreement and settlement. These strategies tend to be contradictory and it is useful for the negotiator to use only one at a time, but it is possible to use a combination. The strategies are outlined briefly below.

Problem solving is the process of creating a formula or alternative option that is conducive to reconciling the interests of both parties. Problem solving can be an individual or joint activity between the two parties and formulae include finding ways to increase resources that have been in short supply, cutting the costs while managing to concede to the other party what is requested, compensation which rewards the other party for its concessions, logrolling in which both parties concede on low priority issues and bridging which satisfies the aims of both parties.

Contending is another name for positional bargaining which has already been described, but Pruitt and Rubin differ with Fisher and Ury (1981) regarding the latter's totally negative assessment of this approach. The former argue that contending can be an important initial stage of discussion that is the required

precursor to successful problem solving. The aspirations of negotiating parties often tend to be so high that no amount of problem
solving will produce a solution which creates a contentious
discussion that leads to more realistic behavior based on diminished aspirations.

Yielding is often the outcome of positional bargaining in that it
leads to reduced demands and aspirations. It is a straightforward
tactic which does not require as much strategizing as problem
solving and contending. The essential guideline for yielding is not
to yield too much and too quickly. Some yielding is positive as it
reduces aspirations, while heavy yielding may also be beneficial
when time pressure exists and the issues involved are unimpor-
tant. Yielding too far and too quickly however, allows the other
party to take the bulk of whatever was contested, leaving the
yielding party with very little. The ideal is for parties to yield to a
point where they can begin to engage in constructive problem
solving.

Inaction is a time wasting strategy and usually leads to a break
in negotiations as does withdrawal. Pruitt and Rubin (1986, 1983)
propose a theoretical model for choosing the above strategies
termed the dual concern model.

The dual concern model makes predictions about the possible
outcomes of utilizing one of the four above mentioned strategies
in conjunction with different levels of concern (i.e. degrees of
high to low). This model predicts and such predictions have been
substantiated by studies that the most successful outcome is a
combination of the problem solving strategy with mutual concern
by both parties. Both parties participated in active problem
solving behavior and their success was measured by the high sum
of their joint profits. The combination of high concern about own
outcomes coupled with low concern about the other party's
interests produced a moderately low sum of the two parties'
profits. Contending behavior was used especially in this form of
negotiation involving both persuasive argument and threat. Finally a low concern about one's own outcome coupled with a high
concern for the other party produced the lowest benefit for both
parties of all combinations and involved yielding on the side of
one of the parties to a low level of aspiration. A low level of
concern from both of the parties produced inaction and a total
lack of joint benefits.

Strategic choice is also influenced according to Pruitt and
Rubin by perceived feasibility and cost. Feasibility may be doubtful for both the strategies of contending and problem solving

because these strategies depend on responses from the other party, while yielding and inaction only depends on one's own behavior. All options however involve some degree of cost. Cost and feasibility supplement considerations specified by the dual concern model because although the latter conditions strategic choice according to the most profitable combinations of concern for joint benefit, the former stresses the minimum requirement for negotiating of minimal feasibility without undue cost. If feasibility is deficient or the cost of a particular combination of strategies is too high, another combination of strategies will be chosen even if they produce lowered joint or one-sided benefits.

In relation to problem solving this strategy would be the most feasible depending on the level of perceived common ground (PCG). PCG which is the potential for finding mutually acceptable agreement, increases when both parties have lowered aspirations and believe that alternatives exist which can bring mutual agreement to both parties. When both parties know that an alternative exists that is mutually satisfactory PCG is maximal and costs will be lowest.

Contending appears the most feasible course of action when one party has strong feelings which represents a lowered resistance to yielding. Cost can be high with contentious behavior as in severe forms a risk of alienating the other party and causing escalating conflicts exists. Costs can also be controlled in using this strategy by constituent surveillance which pressures the negotiating party to be either tough or conciliatory.

Inaction wastes the most time and is the least feasible and holds the highest costs especially in the case of time-pressured decision making. Inaction may be extremely expensive in the case of the negotiated object being perishable goods that could be lost because of delaying tactics. Pruitt and Rubin maintain therefore that the three coping strategies are the most useful for successful negotiation and that they work the most efficiently under conditions of time pressure. Yielding is the quickest way to reach agreement, but contending and problem solving will be adopted in the case of strong resistance to yielding.

DEVIATIONS FROM RATIONALITY—A PROBLEM OF NEGOTIATOR JUDGMENT

Until this point, it has been assumed by the previously reviewed theorists that all negotiators whether using BATNAS or strategic choices will make rational decisions. Bazerman (1983) points out that the rational judgment of negotiators can not be relied upon as they have their limitations. As prescriptive strategies encourage the increased performance of negotiators, Bazerman argues that negotiators can be trained to overcome their tendency to deviate from rationality and he points to five ways in which this deviation from rationality may occur.

The first problem that many negotiators face is how they represent the contexual framework of the negotiations. The importance of framing negotiations positively may be seen through studies such as those by Kahneman and Tversky (1979) which show that individuals will pursue risk-averse behavior when individuals are evaluating gains and risk-seeking behavior when they are evaluating loses. Negotiators need to evaluate the influence of both positive and negative frames, leading the other party to a positive frame of reference by concentrating on what the other party has to gain. An additional rational course for the negotiator would be making it clear to the other party that they are in a risky situation in respect to sure gain, causing individuals to pursue risk-averse behavior.

The fixed pie assumption of the distributive model is another fundamental false assumption that hinders negotiators finding creative (integrative) solutions. The idea that a fixed pie always exists with one party of necessity the loser, while the other the winner claiming the bulk of the pie is a mental distortion because most conflict resolution in reality depends on trade-offs which rely on creative solutions making both parties "winners."

Negotiators often fall into the trap of believing that they have invested too much in a cause which makes them more intrangient and causes an escalation of the conflict. Therefore, it is important for the negotiator to be aware of their own behavior which would induce the other party to believe that they have invested too much too quit or lower aspirations. To accomplish this effectively, the negotiator is required to evaluate constantly the benefits and costs of the present stage of conflict, avoid escalating commitment further to a previous inflamatory course of action, think in terms of future costs and benefits, not past ones and avoid escalating conflict to justify past actions.

Overconfidence is another less than rational tendency which negotiators succumb to believing that their judgment is infallible and that they will win if they maintain their position. Research undertaken by Bazerman shows that negotiators tend to overestimate the probability that under final offer arbitration their final offer will be accepted by both the arbitrator and the other party.

Negotiators need to be aware that overconfidence tends to occur in cases where a party's knowledge is limited and that they must seek to reduce if not eliminate such overconfidence if negotiations are to be successful.

Finally, negotiators often irrationally forget that when the other party accepts their offer it is usually least desirable to the negotiator making the offer. Negotiators need to remind themselves that they are at a disadvantage when they are dealing with an informed opponent who may be too willing to make an agreement because they have the necessary information to judge that acceptance of the offer will be advantageous to themselves. Negotiators therefore, need, through perhaps expert advice, the knowledge they lack to balance information in negotiations.

MEDIATED NEGOTIATION

Mediation discussed at the beginning of this chapter has a role to play in negotiation. Mediation when discussed within the context of negotiation is different from strict mediation processes mentioned at the beginning of this chapter. Such negotiation has been described as the mediation of negotiation or mediated negotiation (Susskind and Ozawa 1983; Raiffa 1982). This process refers to a neutral intervenor who may be invited or may be the invitee to encourage dispute resolution between a number of parties. Raiffa (1982) points out that negotiators hold two basic attitudes toward third party intervention. One is viewing the intervenor as someone to rely on for added advice and support if bargaining between the negotiating parties does not succeed. Intervenors on the other hand, may be perceived as a threat in the case of an intrangient negotiator who may be pressured into being more reasonable because of the threat of third party intervention in an unknown perhaps unpleasant way. The presence of a neutral intervenor introduces new dimensions to the negotiations and causes negotiators to review their tactical options in relation to cooperation, disclosure of facts and so forth. The decision to invite or accept an invitation from a third party therefore is a complex decision that presents many uncertainties.

THE ROLE OF THE MEDIATOR IN NEGOTIATIONS

Mediators within the negotiation process may be involved in a continuum of roles ranging from weak to strong. In weaker, more simple negotiations, the mediator may be a neutral discussion leader chairing discussions to maintain order. In more complex, stronger negotiations, the mediator has a more involved role in preparing impartial minutes of the meetings, summarizing or articulating any perceived consensus. The mediator may not be involved in actual negotiations, but facilitate agreement in a number of ways such as preparing public relations documents that explain clearly the need for compromise, by attesting for the good faith of the negotiators making it clear that no secret agreements were reached, helping to verify the present agreements and aid in future grievances related to ambiguities in the contract. In addition the mediator may seek to improve the atmosphere of negotiations in assisting with personal problems, by helping to stabilize and control emotions and help direct the parties towards conciliation rather than conflict.

In some circumstances the mediator has to serve as the initiator of negotiations, especially in escalating conflicts in which one side refuses to negotiate and the other side feels its offer to negotiate would be interpreted as a sign of weakness. Intervenors may also take the initiative in multiparty disputes when it would be inappropriate for disputants to select which parties or issues should be negotiated. Raiffa (1983, 1982) notes further that mediators within the negotiational context can be especially helpful in situations of intensity and complexity that require additional analytical skills. He believes that negotiating parties could benefit from putting aside their competitiveness and allowing a mediator to help analyze the joint problems and devise creative alternatives.

THE ATTRACTIONS OF MEDIATED NEGOTIATION

Mediated negotiation, which was defined earlier, is being used increasingly as a form of mediation to deal with complex issues in relation to community, environmental, intergovernmental, scientific and family disputes. Recently, it has also been used to supplement traditional institutionalized judicial, administrative and legislative decision making (Talbot 1983, Goldmann 1980). Face-to-face negotiation that is aided by a neutral third party or intervenor has been used in relation to state unemployment compensation funds, hazardous waste policies and other public sector issues that go far beyond interpersonal disputes between neighbors or husbands and wives.

Susskind and Ozawa (1983) argue that mediated negotiation is attractive because it circumvents many of the obstacles provided by conventional, institutional dispute resolution procedures. Mediated negotiation allows for those most affected by the dispute to be directly involved and it produces results more rapidly and at a lower cost than do courts. This type of negotiation is far more flexible and adaptable to the specific requirements of the participants. Mediated negotiation has the potential to be especially helpful in public disputes.

Mediated negotiation within the context of public sector disputes can be a very useful form of negotiation as the mediators are accountable to the public interest at large. This crucial point of accountability can be achieved if mediators; a) follow an activist model of negotiation which involves them actively in the development of dispute settlement, b) they adopt a method of procedure that is appropriate to the situation of negotiation and which is known to all the participants, c) they hold general standards of success which emphasize the quality of the agreement rather than the substance of each particular case d) they continue to seek ways for overcoming obstacles to the widespread use of mediated negotiation in the public sector such as ways to clearly identify all legitimate interests in the conflict, lack of publicity concerning the availability of mediation methods and a lack of trained mediators.

Susskind and Ozawa (1983), in making the above points, find that the international model of negotiation is more closely aligned to their idea of sound mediated negotiation. In contrast to the traditional labor model of negotiation (or collective bargaining) in which the mediator is primarily concerned with the process rather than the quality of results, the international model facilitates concern with both the process and the outcome. The international model also allows active negotiation on the mediator's part which often facilitates conflict resolution through offering inducements or simply pointing out the benefits or harm of a particular solution. The mediator therefore in the international model maintains direct control over the proceedings and actively contributes to a fair solution.

Henry Kissinger is put forward as an exemplary mediator in negotiated settlement (Rubin 1981) because he; a) directly controlled all communications between the disputing parties, b) actively persuaded the parties to make concessions, c) acted as a scapegoat and deflector of the parties' anger and frustration, rather than allowing the parties to express their emotions to one another, d) coordinated the exchange of concessions, and, by so doing masked the bargaining strengths of the parties to one another, e) made his own proposals for possible resolution, and f) created and maintained the momentum of the talks (Susskind and Ozawa, 1983:272–3).

Such strategy coupled with Fisher's prescriptions for exerting influence and balancing power differentials outlined earlier can produce effective, fair and powerful negotiating capabilities in negotiators and mediators in a negotiated mediation.

References

Abel, Richard, *The Politics of Informal Justice,* New York: Academic Press, 1982.

————, "Conservative Conflict and the Reproduction of Capitalism", *International Journal of the Sociology of Law,* 1981, pp. 248–260.

Bazerman, M. H., "Negotiator Judgement: A Critical Look at the Rationality Assumption", *American Behavioral Scientist* (known hereon as *ABS*), Vol. 27, No. 2 1983, pp. 211–229.

Becker, Howard, *Man in Reciprocity,* New York: Praeger, 1956.

Becker, Howard S., *Outsiders: Studies in the Sociology of Deviance,* New York: The Free Press, 1963.

Blalock, Hubert, *Toward a Theory of Minority Group Relations,* New York: John Wiley, 1967.

Bonacich, Edna, "A Theory of Middlemen Theories", *American Sociological Review,* Vol. 38, 1973, pp. 583–594.

Fisher, Roger, "Negotiating Power: Getting and Using Influence", *ABS,* Vol. 27, No. 2, 1983, pp. 149–167.

Fisher, Roger and William Ury, *Getting to Yes: Negotiating Agreement Without Giving In,* New York: Penguin Books, 1981.

Goldman, Robert B. (ed.), *Roundtable Justice: Case Studies in Conflict Resolution,* Boulder, CO: Westview Press, 1980.

Hofrichter, R., "Neighborhood Justice and Social Control Problems of American Capitalism", in Richard Abel, *The Politics of Informal Justice,* New York: Academic Press, 1982.

Kahneman, D. and A. Tversky, "Prospect Theory: An Analysis of Decision Under Risk," *Econometrica,* Vol. 47, 1979, pp. 263–291.

Laue, James, "Conflict Intervention" in Marvin Olsen and M. Micklin, *Handbook of Applied Sociology,* New York: Praeger, 1981.

Mills. C. Wright, *White Collar,* New York: Oxford University Press, 1959.

Moore, Barrington, *Terror and Progress: USSR,* Cambridge: Harvard University Press, 1954.

Park, Robert, *Race and Culture,* New York: The Free Press, 1950.

Patton, Bruce, *On Teaching Negotiation,* Harvard University, Program on Negotiation, Working Paper 85–3, 1985.

Polsky, Ned, *Hustlers, Beats, and Others,* Chicago: Aldine, 1967.

Porter, Jack Nusan, "The Urban Middleman: A Comparative Analysis", *Comparative Social Research,* Vol. 4, 1981, pp. 199–215.

Pruitt, Dean G., "Strategic Choices in Negotiation", *ABS,* Vol. 27, 2, 1983, pp. 167–195.

Pruitt, Dean G. and Jeffrey Z. Rubin, *Social Conflict: Escalation, Stalemate, and Settlement,* New York: Random House, 1986.

Raiffa, Howard, *The Art and Science of Negotiation,* Cambridge, MA: Harvard University Press, 1982.

———, "Mediation of Conflicts", *ABS,* Vol. 27, 2, 1983, pp. 195–211.

Rifkin, Jeremy, "Mediating Disputes: An American Paradox", *Alsa Forum,* Vol. VI, 3, 1982, pp. 263–279.

Rinder, Irwin, "Strangers in the Land: Social Relations in the Status Gap", *Social Problems,* Vol. 6, 1958–1959, pp. 253–260.

Rubin, Jeffrey Z., "Negotiation: An Introduction to Some Issues and Themes", *ABS,* Vol. 27, 2, 1983, pp. 135–149.

———, *Dynamics of Third Party Intervention: Kissinger in the Middle East,* New York: Praeger, 1981.

Simmel, Georg, *The Sociology of Georg Simmel,* New York: Fress Press, 1964.

Skolnick, Jerome H., *Justice Without Trial,* New York: John Wiley, 1967.

Stryker, Sheldon, "Social Structure and Prejudice", *Social Problems,* Vol. 6, 1959, pp. 340–354.

Susskind, Lawrence and C. Ozawa, "Mediated Negotiation in the Public Sector", *ABS,* Vol. 27, 2, 1983, pp. 255–277.

Susskind, Lawrence and Jeffrey Z. Rubin, Introduction, *ABS,* Vol. 27, 2, 1983, pp. 133–135.

Talbot, A., *Settling Things: Six Case Studies in Environmental Disputes,* Washington, DC: Conservation Foundation, 1983.

Weber, Max, *The Theory of Social and Economic Organization,* New York: The Free Press, 1964.

Selected Readings

General Classical Theory

Bendix, Reinhard, *Max Weber: An Intellectual Portrait,* Garden City: Anchor Books, 1962.

Park, Robert E. and Ernest W. Burgess, *The Introduction to the Science of Society,* Chicago: University of Chicago, 1921.

Park, Robert E., *Race and Culture,* New York: The Free Press, 1950.

Stonequist, Everett V., *The Marginal Man,* New York: Scribner's 1973.

Thomas, W. I. and F. Znaniecki, *The Polish Peasant in Europe and America,* Chicago: University of Chicago, 1918.

Young, Kimball, *The Contribution of William Isaac Thomas,* reproduced from *Sociology and Social Research,* Vol. 47, nos. 1, 2, 3, 4, Los Angeles: University of Southern California Press, 1968.

Weber, Max, *The Theory of Social and Economic Organization,* trans. by A. M. Henderson and T. Parsons, Edited by Talcott Parsons, New York: The Free Press, 1964.

Conflict Theory: Classical and Contemporary

Coser, Lewis, *The Functions of Social Conflict,* New York: The Free Press, 1956.

Coser, Lewis A., "The Termination of Conflict," *Journal of Conflict Resolution,* Vol. 5, December, 1961, pp. 347–353.

Coser, Lewis A. and Bernard Rosenberg, *Sociological Theory: A Book of Readings,* New York: The Macmillan Company, 1966, especially 175–308.

Dahrendorf, Ralf, "Toward a Theory of Social Conflict," *Journal of Conflict Resolution,* Vol. II, No. 2, June, 1958.

Dahrendorf, Ralf, "Out of Utopia: Toward a Reorientation of Sociological Analysis," *American Journal of Sociology,* Vol. LXIV, September, 1958, pp. 115–127.

Dahrendorf, Ralf, *Class and Class Conflict in Industrial Society,* Stanford: Stanford University Press, 1959.

Dahrendorf, Ralf, *Gesellschaft und Freiheit,* Munich: R. Piper and Company, 1961.

Gluckman, Max, *Custom and Conflict in Africa,* New York: The Free Press, 1956.

Gluckman, Max, *Politics, Law, and Ritual in Tribal Society,* Chicago: Aldine Company, 1965.

Gluckman, Max, "The Peace in the Feud," in Lewis Coser and Bernard Rosenberg, *Sociological Theory: A Book of Readings,* New York: Macmillan Company, 1966.

Simmel, Georg, *Conflict and the Web of Group-Affiliations,* (Tr. Kurt H. Wolff and Reinhard Bendix), New York: The Free Press, 1964.

Simmel, Georg, *The Sociology of Georg Simmel,* Kurt H. Wolff (trans.) New York: The Free Press, 1964, Especially pp. 145–169 (The Triad), pp. 216–221 (Subordination Under and Individual) pp. 402–408 (The Stranger) and pp. 409–424 (The Metropolis and Mental Life).

The Sociology of Conflict

Angell, Robert C., "The Sociology of Human Conflict" in Elton McNeil (ed.) *The Nature of Human Conflict,* Englewood Cliffs, NJ: Prentice-Hall, 1965.

Berk, Richard, A., *Collective Behavior,* Dubuque, Iowa: W. C. Brown, 1974.

Bernard, Jessie, "Where is the Modern Sociology of Conflict?" *American Journal of Sociology,* Volume 56, 1950, pp. 111–116.

Coleman, James S., *Community Conflict,* New York: Free Press, 1957.

Collins, Randall, *Conflict Sociology,* New York: Academic Press, 1975.

Denisoff, R. Serge et. al. (eds.) *Theories and Paradigms in Contemporary Sociology,* Itasca, Ill.: F. E. Peacock, 1974, esp. pp. 297–352.

Deutsch, Martin, *The Resolution of Conflict,* New Haven, Ct.: Yale University Press, 1973.

Edari, Ronald S., *Social Change,* Dubuque, Iowa: W. C. Brown, 1976.

Fink, Clinton F., "Some Conceptual Difficulties in the Theory of Social Conflict," *Journal of Conflict Resolution,* Vol. 12, Dec. 1968, pp. 429–431.

Flacks, Richard, *Youth and Social Change,* Chicago: Markham Publishing Company, 1971.

Galtung, Johan, "Institutionalized Conflict Resolution: A Theoretical Paradigm," *Journal of Peace Research,* Volume 2, 1965, pp. 348–396.

Gamson, William, *The Strategy of Social Protest,* Homewood, Ill.: Dorsey Press, 1975.

Gurr, Ted, *Why Men Rebel,* Princeton, NJ: Princeton University Press, 1970.

Horton, John, "Order and Conflict Theories of Social Problems as Competing Ideologies," *American Journal of Sociology,* LXXI, 6, May 1966, pp. 701–713.

Kreisberg, Louis, *The Sociology of Social Conflict,* Englewood Cliffs, NJ: Prentice-Hall, 1973.

Loomis, Charles P., "In Praise of Conflict and its Resolution," *American Sociological Review,* 32, December 1967, pp. 875–890.

Mack, Raymond and Richard C. Snyder, "The Analysis of Social Conflict," *Journal of Conflict Resolution,* Vol. 1, No. 2, June 1957, pp. 212–248.

Oberschall, Anthony, *Social Conflict and Social Movements,* Englewood, Cliffs, NJ: Prentice-Hall, 1973.

Tilly, Charles, "Revolutions and Collective Violence" in Fred Greenstein and Nelson Polsby (eds.), *Handbook of Political Science,* Vol. 3, New York: Addison-Wesley, 1975.

Timasheff, Nicholas, S., *War and Revolution,* New York: Sheed and Ward, 1965.

Williams, Robin M., *Mutual Accommodation: Ethnic Conflict and Cooperation,* Minneapolis, Mn: University of Minnesota Press, 1977.

Situational Theory

Goffman, Erving, *The Presentation of Self in Everyday Life,* Garden City, New York: Doubleday and Company, 1959.

Goffman, Erving, *Encounters,* Indianapolis, Indiana: The Bobbs-Merril Company, Inc., 1961.

Goffman, Erving, Discussion of "Communication and Enforcement Systems" in Kathleen Archibald (ed.), *Strategic Interaction and Conflict: Original Papers and Discussion,* Berkeley, California: Institute of International Studies, International Security Program, 1966, pp. 199–200.

Goffman, Erving, *Interaction Ritual,* Garden City, New York: Anchor Books, 1967.

Small Group Research:
General References

Hare, A. Paul, *Handbook of Small Group Research,* New York: The Free Press, 1962.

Homans, George, *The Human Group,* New York: Harcourt, Brace, and World, Inc., 1950.

Homans, George, *Social Behavior: Its Elementary Forms,* New York: Harcourt, Brace and World, Inc., 1961.

Lewin, Kurt, *Resolving Social Conflicts—Selected Papers on Group Dynamics,* New York: Harpers and Row, 1948.

Mills, Theodore M. *The Sociology of Small Groups,* Englewood Cliffs: New Jersey, 1967. (Esp. pp. 10–24, 123–130.)

Thibaut, J. W. and H. H. Kelley, *The Social Psychology of Groups,* New York: John Wiley and Sons, 1959.

Small Group Research:
The Triad

Caplow, Theodore A., "A Theory of Coalitions in the Triad," *American Sociological Review,* Vol. XXI, 1965, pp. 489–493.

Caplow, Theodore A., "Further Developments of a Theory of Coalitions in the Triad," *American Journal of Sociology,* Vol. 64, 1959, pp. 488–493.

Caplow, Theodore, *Two Against One: Coalitions in Triads,* Englewood Cliffs, N.J.: Prentice-Hall, 1968.

Mills, Theodore M., "Power Relations in Three-Person Groups," *American Sociological Review,* Vol. 18, August, 1953, pp. 351–357.

Mills, Theodore M., "The Coalition Pattern in Three-Person

Groups," *American Sociological Review,* Vol. 19, December, 1954, pp. 657–667.

Mills, Theodore M., "Development Process in Three-Person Groups," *Human Relations,* Vol. 9, 1956, pp. 343–354.

Strodbeck, Fred L., "The Family as a Three-Person Group," *American Sociological Review,* Vol. 19, February, 1954.

Torrance, E. Paul, "Some Consequences of Power Differences on Decision Making in Permanent and Temporary Three-Man Groups," in A. Paul Hare, Edgar F. Horgotta, and Robert F. Bales (editors), *Small Groups: Studies in Social Interaction,* New York: Alfred A. Knopf, 1955, pp. 482–492.

Small Group Research:
Communication, Interaction, and Group Size

Bales, Robert F., "Some Uniformities of Behavior in Small Social Systems," in G. E. Swanson, T. M. Newcomb, and E. L. Hartley, (eds) *Reading in Social Psychology,* New York: Holt, 1952, pp. 146–159.

Bales, Robert F. and Edgar F. Borgotta, "Size of Group as a Factor in the Interaction Profile," in A. Paul Hare, Edgar F. Borgotta and Robert F. Bales (editors), *Small Groups: Studies in Social Interaction,* New York: Alfred A. Knopf, 1955, pp. 396–413.

Bavelas, Alex, "Communication Patterns in Task-Oriented Groups," *Journal of the Acoustical Society of America,* Vol. XX, 1950, pp. 725–730.

Fouriezos, N. T., M. L. Hutt, and Harold Guetzkow, "Measurement of Self-Oriented Need in Discussion Groups," *Journal of Abnormal and Social Psychology,* Vol. 45, 1950, pp. 682–690.

Leavitt, Harold J., "Some Effects of Certain Communication Patterns on Group Performance," *Journal of Abnormal and Social Psychology,* Vol. XLVI, 1951, pp. 38–50.

Newcomb, Theodore M., "An Approach to the Study of Communicative Acts," *The Psychological Review,* Vol. 60, November, 1953, pp. 393–404.

Shaw, M. E., "Some Effects of Problem Complexity Upon Problem Solution Efficiency in Different Communication Nets," *Journal of Experimental Psychology,* Vol. 48, 1954, pp. 211–217.

Small Groups:
Methods of Structured Observation

Bales, Robert, *Interaction Process Analysis,* Cambridge, Mass.: Addison-Wesley, 1950.

Bales, Robert F., "A Set of Categories for the Analysis of Small Group Interaction," *American Sociological Review,* Vol. 15, April, 1950, pp. 257–263.

Mills, Theodore M., *Group Transformation,* Englewood Cliffs, N.J.: Prentice-Hall, 1964.

Stone, Philip J., Dexter C. Dunphy, Marshall S. Smith, and Daniel M. Ogilvie, *The General Inquirer, A Computer Approach to Content Analysis,* Cambridge, Mass.: M.I.T. Press, 1966.

Small Groups:
Bargaining and Negotiation

Praeger, Geoffrey and Jack Sawyer, "The Influence of Knowledge and Normative Information in a Dyadic Bargaining Game," Northwestern University, Psychology Dept., Evanston, Ill., n.d. (mimeographed). approximately 1967.

Sawyer, Jack and Harold Geutzkow, "Bargaining and Negotiations in International Relations," in Herbert C. Kelman (editor), *International Behavior: a Social-Psychological Analysis,* New York: Holt, Rinehart, and Winston, 1965.

Sawyer, Jack, "Experiments in the Resolution of Interpersonal Conflict," Psychology Dept., Northwestern University, Evanston, Ill., April, 1966 (mimeographed).

Wells, Roger B. *Control of Disruptive Behavior in a Bargaining Game,* Unpublished Ph.D. thesis, University of North Carolina, Psychology Dept., Chapel Hill, North Carolina, 1967.

Mediation of Group Conflict

Boulding, Kenneth E., *Conflict and Defense: A General Theory,* New York: Harper and Row, 1962, (esp. Chapter on "Conflict Resolution and Control" pp. 305–328).

Chase, Stuart, *Roads to Agreement: Successful Methods in the Science of Human Relations,* London: Phoenix House Ltd., 1952, and New York: Harper & Brothers, 1951.

Douglas, Ann, *Industrial Peacemaking,* New York: Columbia University Press, 1962. (esp. pp. 2–199)

Gulliver, P. H., *Disputes and Negotiations,* New York, Academic Press, 1979.

Indik, Bernard P., Bernard Goldstein, Jack Chernik, Monroe Berkovitz, *The Mediator: Background, Self-Image, and Attitudes,* New Brunswick, New Jersey: Research Program, Institute of Management and Labor Relations, Rutgers—The State University, 1966.

Kahn-Freund, O., "Intergroup Conflicts and their Settlement," *The British Journal of Sociology,* Vol. 5, No. 3, Sept., 1954, pp. 193–227.

Kerr, Clark, "Industrial Conflict and its Mediation," *American Journal of Sociology,* Vol. 60, Vol. 3, November, 1954.

Lewin, Kurt, *Resolving Social Conflicts,* New York: Harper and Brothers, 1948.

Meynaud, Jean et Brigitte Schroder, *La Mediation: Tendances de la Recherche et Bibliographie* (1945–1959), Vol. II, Survey of Research in the Social Science, Amsterdam: North Holland Publishing Company, 1961.

Odiorne, G. S., "Arbitration and Mediation Among Early Quakers," *The Arbitration Journal,* Vol. 9, No. 3, 1954, pp. 161–166.

Rose, Arnold M., *Group Conflict and its Mediation: Hypotheses for Research,* Association Internationale de Sociologie, Congres de Liege, 1953, 2e section (and other papers as well).

Williams, Robin M., *The Reduction of Intergroup Tensions,* New York: Social Science Research Council, Bulletin 57, 1947.

Witty, Cathie J., *Mediation and Society,* New York: Academic Press, 1980.

Game Theory

Archibald, Kathleen (editor), *Strategic Interaction and Conflict: Original Papers and Discussion,* Berkeley, Calif.: Institute of International Studies, International Security Program, 1966.

Buckley, Walter, (editor), *Modern Systems Research for the Behavioral Scientist: A Source book,* Chicago: Aldine Co., 1968, (Esp. pp. 3–38, 123–142, 387–400, 475–513).

Cohen, Albert K., "The Study of Social Disorganization and Deviant Behavior" in Robert K. Merton, et. al., *Sociology*

Today, Problems and Prospects, New York: Basic Books, pp. 475–479.

Long, Norton E., "The Local Community as an Ecology of Games," *The American Journal of Sociology,* Vol. LXIV, November, 1958, pp. 251–261.

Luce, R. Duncan and Howard Raiffa, *Games and Decisions,* New York: John Wiley, 1957.

Rapoport, Anatol and Albert M. Chammah, *Prisoner's Dilemma: A Study in Conflict and Cooperation,* Ann Arbor, Michigan Press, 1965.

Rapoport, Anatol, *Two-Person Game Theory: The Essential Ideas,* Ann Arbor: University of Michigan Press, 1966.

Schelling, Thomas, *The Strategy of Conflict,* Cambridge, Mass.: Harvard University Press, 1960.

Shubik, M., (ed.) *Game Theory and Related Approaches to Social Behavior,* New York: John Wiley, 1964, paper.

Von Neumann, John and Oskar Morgenstern, *Theory of Games and Economic Behavior,* New York: John Wiley, 3rd. ed., paper, 1964.

Simulation and Model Construction

Beshers, J. M., "Model and Theory Construction," *American Sociological Review,* Vol XXII, 1957, pp. 32–38.

Broadbeck, May, "Models, Meaning, and Theories," in L. Gross (ed.), *Symposium on Sociological Theory,* Evanston, Ill.,: Row, Peterson, 1959, pp. 373–403.

Coleman, James S., *Introduction to Mathematical Sociology,* New York: The Free Press, 1964.

Coleman, James S. "Mathematical Models and Computer Simulation," in R. E. L. Faris (ed.) *Handbook of Modern Sociology,* Chicago: Rand McNally, 1964.

Guetzkow, Harold, (ed.) *Simulation in Social Science: Readings,* Englewood Cliffs, New Jresey: Prentice-Hall, 1962.

Guetzkow, Harold, et. al., *Simulation in International Relations: Developments for Research and Teaching,* Englewood Cliffs, New Jersey: Prentice-Hall, 1963.

Richardson, Lewis, F., *Statistics of Deadly Quarrels,* Chicago: Quadrangle, 1960.

Richardson, Lewis F., "The Statistics of Deadly Quarrels" in Alex Inkeles (ed.), *Readings on Modern Sociology,* Englewood Cliffs, N.J.: Prentice-Hall, 1966.

Simon, Herbert, *Models of Man: Social and Rational*, New York: John Wiley, 1957.

Miscellaneous Reference Works:
Theoretical Perspectives

Gouldner, Alvin W., *The Coming Crisis of Western Sociology*, New York: Avon Books, 1970.

Greer, Scott, *The Logic of Social Inquiry*, Chicago: Aldine Publishing Company, 1969. (pp. 144–145, 165–167).

Inkeles, Alex, *What is Sociology?* Englewood Cliffs, New Jersey: Prentice-Hall, 1964.

Martindale, Don, *The Nature and Types of Sociological Theory*, Boston, Mass.: Houghton-Mifflin, 1960.

Merton, Robert K., *Social Theory and Social Structure*, (rev. and enlarged ed.), New York: The Free Press, 1967.

Tiryakian, Edward A., *Sociologism and Existentialism: Two Perspectives on the Individual and Society*, Englewood Cliffs, N.J.: Prentice-Hall, 1962.

Wrong, Dennis, "The Oversocialized Conception of Man," *American Sociological Review*, Vol. XXVI, 1961, pp. 183–192.

Varieties of Middleman: Background Material

Anderson, Stanley V., *Canadian Ombudsman Proposals*, Berkeley, California: Institute of Governmental Studies, 1966.

Becker, Howard S., *Outsiders: Studies in the Sociology of Deviance*, New York: The Free Press, 1963 (Esp., pp. 20, 159–161).

Bordua, David J., (editor), "The Police" *Six Sociological Essays*, New York: John Wiley and Sons, 1967.

Hughes, Everett and Helen M. Hughes, *Where Peoples Meet*, New York: The Free Press, 1952.

Hurwitz, Stephan, *The Ombudsman*, Copenhagen, Denmark: Det Danske Selskab, 1962.

Moore, Barrington, *Terror and Progress: U.S.S.R.:* Cambridge: Harvard University Press, 1954.

Polsky, Ned, *Hustlers, Beats, and Others*, Chicago: Aldine Publishing Co., 1967.

Redlinger, Lawrence J., *Market Mechanisms and Distribution Patterns of Illicit Drugs*, unpublished manuscript, Northwestern University, 1968.

Skolnick, Jerome H., *Justice Without Trial: Law Enforcement in Democratic Society,* New York: John Wiley and Sons, 1967. (Esp. pp. 42–70, 116, 124).

Wilson, James Q., *Varieties of Police Behavior,* Cambridge, Mass.: Harvard University Press, 1968.

Types of Middlemanship

Becker, Howard, *Man in Reciprocity,* New York: Frederick A. Praeger, 1956.

Boulding, Kenneth E., *Conflict and Defense: A General Theory,* New York: Harper and Row, 1962, Esp. pp. 305–328.

Chinoy, Eli, *Society,* New York, Random House, 1967, pp. 100–101.

Dun and Bradstreet, Inc. *The Failure Record Through 1966: A Comprehensive Study of Business Failures,* New York: Dun and Bradstreet, Inc. 1967.

Gosnell, Harold F., *Machine Politics: Chicago Model,* Chicago: University of Chicago Press, 1937.

Mack, Raymond (ed.), *Race, Class, and Power,* New York: American Book Co., 1963, p. 287.

Marden, Charles F. and Gladys Meyer, *Minorities in American Society,* 2nd edition, New York: American Book Company, 1962, pp. 413, 422–440, 441–465.

Mayer, Kurt B. and Sidney Goldstein, *The First Two Years: Problems of Small Firm Growth and Survival.* Washington, D.C.: Small Business Administration, 1961.

Mills, C. Wright, *White Collar,* New York: Oxford University Press, 1959, pp. 91–100.

Park, Robert E., *Race and Culture,* New York: The Free Press, 1950, 194–195.

Polsky, Ned, *Hustlers, Beats, and Others,* Chicago, Aldine Publishing Company, 1967.

Porter, Jack Nusan, "The Urban Middleman: A Cross-Cultural Approach," *Comparative Social Research,* JAI Press, Vol. 4, 1981.

Rinder, Irwin, "Strangers in the Land: Social Relations in the Status Gap," *Social Problems,* Vol. 6, (1958–59), pp. 253–260.

Sombart, Werner, *The Jews and Modern Capitalism,* New York: The Free Press, 1951.

Stonequist, Everett V., *The Marginal Man,* New York: Scribner's, 1937.

Sutton, Francis, et. al., *The American Business Creed,* Cambridge: Harvard University Press, 1956.

Wallant, Edward Lewis, *The Pawnbroker,* New York: Mcfadden Books, 1961.

Weber, Max, *The Theory of Social and Economic Organization,* trans. by A. M. Henderson and T. Parsons, edited by Talcott Parsons, New York: The Free Press, 1964, p. 239.

Winch, Robert F. and Rae Lesser Blumberg, "Societal Complexity and Familial Organization" in Robert F. Winch and Louis Wolf Goodman (eds.), *Selected Studies in Marriage and the Family,* New York: Holt, Rinehart and Winston, 1968, (Esp. p. 85).

Wirth, Louis, *The Ghetto,* Chicago: The University of Chicago Press, 1956.

Mediation and Negotiation: New Approaches

American Behavioral Scientist, special issue on negotiation and conflict resolution, Vol. 27, No. 2, 1983.

Bercovitch, J., *Social Conflicts and Third Parties; Strategies of Conflict Resolution,* Boulder, CO: Westview Press, 1984.

Boulding, Elise, J. Robert Passmore, and Robert Scott Gassler, *Bibliography On World Conflict and Peace,* Second Edition, Boulder, CO: Westview Press, 1979.

Brockner, J. and J. Z. Rubin, *The Social Psychology of Conflict: Escalation and Entrapment,* New York: Springer-Verlag, 1985.

Dugan, M. A., (ed.), *Peace and Change,* Special issue on conflict resolution, Volume 8, 1982.

Fisher, Roger, "Negotiation Power: Getting and Using Influence," *ABS,* Vol. 27, No. 2, 1983, pp. 149–167.

————, "Third Party Consultation as a Method of Intergroup Conflict Resolution," *Journal of Conflict Resolution,* Vol. 27, 1983, pp. 301–334.

Fisher, Roger and William Ury, *Getting to Yes: Negotiating Agreements Without Giving In,* New York: Penguin Books, 1981.

Goldman, Robert B. (ed.), *Roundtable Justice: Case Studies in Conflict Resolution,* Boulder, CO: Westview Press, 1980.

Gulliver, P. H., *Disputes and Negotiations; A Cross-Cultural Perspective,* New York: Academic Press, 1979.

Laue, James, "Conflict Intervention" in Marvin Olsen and M.

Micklin, *Handbook of Applied Sociology,* New York: Praeger, 1981.

Patton, Bruce, *On Teaching Negotiation,* Harvard University, Program on Negotiation, Working Paper 85-3, 1985.

Porter, Jack Nusan, "The Urban Middleman: A Comparative Analysis," *Comparative Social Research,* Vol. 4, 1981, pp. 199–215.

Porter, Jack Nusan, *Conflict and Conflict Resolution,* New York: Garland Publishing Company, 1982.

Pruitt, Dean G., "Strategic Choices in Negotiation," *ABS,* Vol. 27, 2, 1983, pp. 167–195.

———, *Negotiation Behavior,* New York: Academic Press, 1981.

Pruitt, Dean G. and Jeffrey Z. Rubin, *Social Conflict: Escalation, Stalemate and Settlement,* New York: Random House, 1986.

Raiffa, Howard, *The Art and Science of Negotiation,* Cambridge, MA: Harvard University Press, 1982.

———, "Mediation of Conflicts," *ABS,* Vol. 27, 2, 1983, pp. 195–211.

Rifkin, Jeremy, "Mediating Disputes: An American Paradox," *Alsa Forum,* Vol. VI, 3, 1982, pp. 263–279.

Rubin, Jeffrey Z., "Negotiation: An Introduction to Some Issues and Themes," *ABS,* Vol. 27, 2, 1983, pp. 135–149.

———, *Dynamics of Third Party Intervention: Kissinger in the Middle East,* New York: Praeger, 1981.

Rubin, Jeffrey Z. and Bert R. Brown, *The Social Psychology of Bargaining and Negotiation,* New York: Academic Press, 1975.

Susskind, Lawrence and C. Ozawa, "Mediated Negotiation in the Public Sector," *ABS,* Vol. 27, 2, 1983, pp. 255–277.

Susskind, Lawrence and Jeffrey Z. Rubin, Introduction, *ABS,* Vol. 27, 2, 1983, pp. 133–135.

Talbot, A., *Settling Things: Six Case Studies in Environmental Disputes,* Washington, DC: Conservation Foundation, 1983.

Touval, S. and I. W. Zartman (eds.), *The Man in the Middle: International Mediation in Theory and Practice,* Boulder, CO: Westview Press, 1985.

Wehr, Paul, *Conflict Regulation,* Boulder, CO: Westview Press, 1979.

About the Authors

Dr. Jack Nusan Porter received his Ph.D. from Northwestern University in sociology in 1971. He has published 20 books and over 200 articles, including *Conflict and Conflict Resolution: A Historical Bibliography* (Garland, 1982), *Readings in Sociology, The Jew as Outsider,* and *Genocide and Human Rights.* He is the founder of the *Journal of the History of Sociology* and the *Sociology of Business Newsletter,* and has lectured at Northwestern University, Boston College, University of Lowell, and most recently was a research fellow at Harvard University. Today, he is President of The Spencer Group of Newton Highlands, Mass., a real estate developing, consulting, and education firm.

Dr. Ruth Taplin received her Ph.D. degree from the London School of Economics in 1984. She has written a number of publications in the field of international development and has lectured at City of London Polytechnic and San Jose State University. Currently, she lectures at Kingston Polytechnic, London, England.